DISRUPTION OFF

The Technological Disruption Coming
For Your Company and What To Do About It

TERRY JONES

This book is dedicated to my wife, Ginny.

She is always supportive of my work
no matter where in the world it takes me.

TABLE OF CONTENTS

INTRODUCTION

> "How did you go bankrupt?"
> "Two ways, gradually and then suddenly!"
>
> —Mike Campbell in *The Sun Also Rises*

About six years ago my wife and I decided to buy a second home in San Clemente, California, to be near our four grown children in the summer.

As I'm travelling almost every week, and at peak times LAX airport is two hours from home, I needed to find a car service for those 6 a.m. departures and midnight arrivals.

At that time Uber wasn't a thing yet in my area, so I found a local firm. They were prompt and efficient, with great drivers. On those long trips, the drivers and I got to know each other pretty well. As they learned my background, they began to complain that they had no technology. All they had was phone and paper.

After several months, one of the drivers said, "I was telling my boss about your bio and he asked if you'd review our website."

Now, normally I'd charge a hefty consulting fee to "look at someone's website," but it was a small organization and I thought, "Well, here I am starting a trip to Outer Mongolia [literally!] for the US Department of State to help small businesses. Why shouldn't I help this one?"

My first impression was that the website was beautiful. Lots of well-shot photos of limos and glitterati, so it had a nice look. But there was way too much pompous text stating things like, "The choice of your limo is the most important factor in your travel experience" (NOT!).

What was worse, the site didn't have pricing and there was no way to book online. They never mentioned safety or promptness, or the fact that every driver called you the night before to reconfirm. So, I wrote my review and my rating was abysmal.

I sent it off and never received a reply.

Six months later, my driver happened to be the owner of the firm. I was curious why I'd never heard back from him, so I said, "You know, I spent a lot of time on that website review you asked for. Was there a reason you didn't respond?"

"You hurt my feelings," he said, "We spent a lot of money on that site and I didn't agree with your conclusions."

"Ok," I replied, then decided to dive in, "Tell me, why don't you have pricing on the website?"

"I want people to call me; I want to build a relationship with them."

"Ed, I understand, but this is the 21st century; people don't call! Can you imagine Travelocity with no pricing or booking ability! Aren't you comfortable stating your prices?"

"Well, we are more expensive than many of our competitors, but we have better service and I want to explain that."

"Look, Ed, I'm worried about your business. You don't have an app, and your confirmation is a PDF that looks like a contract. I can't book on the web. I have to find your driver in a sea of people in baggage claim and he holds a sign written on the back of his daughter's homework! This just isn't going to work for you long-term.

"Here is what I suggest. Build a new website. Call it San Clemente OnLine Limo. Put up pricing and a way to book online and try it out. You can use the same cars and the same drivers. It probably won't cost you $10,000 to experiment. Try it and see which method wins. Old customers who like booking by phone can stay with that approach, and new customers will see an easy-to-use forward-looking company."

"I don't know," he said, obviously conflicted.

"Ed," I asked, "How old are you?"

"55."

I thought about whether to let him know I thought he was making a myopic decision, and decided to go ahead in the hopes it might serve as a wakeup call. "That's too bad, because I don't think you will own this company when you are 65 if you don't change."

The trip ended in silence.

That conversation took place four years ago. I'm sad to say, I got a notice last week that Ed's company had folded.

As the saying goes, "What got you here won't get you there."

And that is why I'm a man on a mission about this topic.

As business owners, executives, and entrepreneurs, if we don't stay alert to the disruptions in and around our industry, we will be out of business or out of job.

Ed had an easy choice. He could have spent a fraction of what he spent on a stretch limo to try and stave off Uber, but he chose to stick with his outdated business model.

Most companies face much harder choices, but his example shows that many companies don't take action until it is just too late.

It could be activist shareholder pressure, quarterly earnings, or regulation that's holding back change. But in my experience, it is much more likely to be inertia, tunnel vision, and comfort with "the known."

This book will try to help you look forward and see the future that is coming for your company, your employees, and your customers.

It will explain my view of the most important technologies and business models that are likely to disrupt your business.

And then it will outline steps you can take now so you don't end up like Ed's limo company.

These are steps any company can and should take to be flexible enough to keep up with the pace of 21st-century disruption.

This isn't an infallible cookbook of certainty. As a budding cook I can tell you that a cookbook from the best chef isn't enough to guarantee a great dish!

However, there are a surprising number of 100-year-old companies out there. And most of the ones I've talked to seem to have mastered the ability to shed their old skin and renew themselves (often quite painfully) when required.

"Don't forget we were founded as an express shipping company," Ken Chenault, the Chairman of American Express, told me, "I don't know what we will be next, but I suspect it could be as far from financial services as financial services are from shipping!"

Ginny Rometty, the CEO of IBM, said, "Don't ever protect your past."

That's one of the goals of this book: to prevent you from protecting your past – and to prepare you to be more proactive about your future.

This book is designed to be "snackable." The chapters don't have to be read in order. You can pick out the sections that seem most applicable to your business and just read those. But read them all if you have time, and then go online and research other disruptive technologies that may be affecting your industry, because as fast as I can write about technologies… they change!

A word of caution: you may have a "EUREKA" moment while reading about a technology and want to rush off and act on it.

That's great, but do that after you read the last section of the book. That's where I go into prescriptive details and recommended next steps that can save you trial and terror learning.

Ready to be updated on the evolution of disruption and how it affects you? Onward!

"All I'm saying is <u>now</u> is the time to develop the technology to deflect an asteroid."

DISRUPTION OFF

"There comes a time in your life when you have
to open the door and let the future in."

—Graham Greene

Disruption. Everyone is talking about it. It is the headline of countless articles, the keynote topic of hundreds of conferences. The question is, how will it affect your business, and what can you do about it.

This book is a companion to my book "ON Innovation" where I outline a series of practical strategies to create more usable, profitable products in your company.

While that book has been well received, my global work in speaking and consulting since then has revealed that something was missing.

And that something became the "burning platform" for this book.

It was time to tell the story of the new technologies and new business models that are impacting industries today, and to discuss strategies that any company can use to mitigate disruption – and leverage it to their advantage.

The thesis of this book? Disruption is coming and coming for almost every business.

Disruption is a topic I know quite a bit about.

As founder of Travelocity – the earliest and for many years the largest online travel site – I led the team that started the online travel revolution. Travel is now far and away the industry most penetrated by online commerce. It is larger than the next three categories of retail *combined!* Online travel booking caused the number of travel agents to shrink from 40,000 to less than 13,000 today.

After Travelocity, I helped disrupt travel again as a cofounder of Kayak.com where we created the Meta Search model and took quite a bit of share from Expedia and Priceline (and became a company that was eventually sold for $1.8 billion).

To understand why disruption is such an important topic today, a look back might help. Historians tell us that the spear was the first implement used for fishing and that occurred about 85,000 years ago. It took almost 40,000 years to get from the spear to the net. Another 20,000 years for the fishhook to appear, and it wasn't until 6,000 years ago that the barbed hook made its appearance.

So about 80,000 years from the spear to the barbed hook! That was innovation then. And the example says nothing about the distribution of the idea, how long did it take the hook to travel from the land of the inventor to the rest of the world. I suspect a very, very long time.

Well you might say that was the ancient world; innovation clearly happens faster now.

You'd be correct! Think of the period from 1850 to 1900. Travel moved from the speed of a horse to the speed of a locomotive. Communication went from the speed of a wagon or sail to the speed of light. Light itself went from a flickering flame to the electric lamp. And production went from muscle power to steam power, which had an exponential effect on output.

And yet even with these great inventions, the electric light, the telegraph, the transcontinental railroad, and industrial steam engine, innovation was unevenly distributed. Although Edison demonstrated his bulb in 1879, by 1925 only half the US population had access to electric light and even by 1932 only 10% of US farms had electricity.

The speed of innovation is different today. While it took 75 years for the telephone to reach 100 million users, Pokémon Go took 15 days!

Think about that … 75 years … 15 days.

What has contributed to that dramatic difference? Connectivity.

With 51% of the world population connected to the Internet, innovation itself now disperses at the speed of light.

And if you think disruption is happening in unrelated industries and won't impact you, think again.

I was speaking in Cincinnati and saw this photo on the wall in my hotel.

I thought about how quickly those paddle wheel steamers disappeared with the invention of the diesel engine and the completion of the transcontinental railroad.

But then I took a closer look. In the background you see a copper shop, a blacksmith shop, a boiler yard, and a steamboat paint shop. They probably all went away too. Perhaps the steamboat paint shop saw it coming, but did the copper shop and the boiler yard? Had they become overly dependent on the status quo and enjoyed the good times without thinking about how quickly things were changing?

Perhaps a more current example can drive the point home.

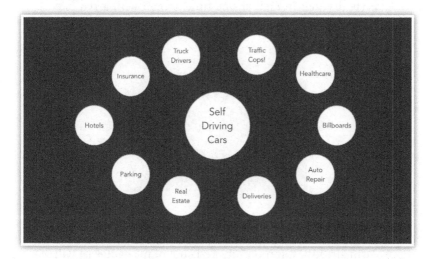

Articles abound on the impact of self-driving electric vehicles, and it is easy to imagine the effect it will have on truck drivers (which is the most popular job in 29 states).[1]

But think of all the other impacts.

- Insurance

    Today, Tesla claims that its self-driving features make its cars 6.7 TIMES safer to drive than others. NHTSA rated the Tesla Model X "perfect," the only car ever given that safety rating.

Although the complexity of these cars (and difficulty to repair) has raised some insurance rates, overall the actuarial tables based on actual performance should produce much lower rates.

On the other hand, when the inevitable crashes do occur, who will bear the liability – the "driver" (read passenger) or the manufacturer?

Expect lots of lawsuits until this is sorted out. In fact, this is one area where it would be great to see government action *before* the disaster. It took quite a long time for the invention of the stop light to bring order to the chaos of early driving. In fact, at one time, a man with a red flag preceded cars driving in cities to avoid scaring horse-driven carriages!

- Parking

I can already "summon" my Tesla out of my garage (it will open the garage door and back itself out), but soon I will be able to tell it to go park itself and call it back when I want it.

How will this affect the design of office buildings and downtown real estate? Will I simply send my car home and schedule it to come back at the end of the workday? Or will I send it to some inexpensive place to park, miles away?

- Auto Repair

  Estimates are that electric vehicles cost one-third to one-half as much to maintain as internal combustion cars, mostly due to dramatically fewer moving parts.

  Service and parts represent 13% of average dealer revenue but *over 40% of gross profit*. No wonder auto dealers are fighting so hard to keep Tesla from selling cars via the Internet, which is prohibited in 11 states and limited to one or two stores in many others. Forty-eight states have laws prohibiting manufacturers from selling cars directly.

- Gas Stations

  Over 80% of gas stations in the US are also convenience stores. Operators can make as much profit on a $2.00 cup of coffee as they do on a $50.00 tank of gas. So why aren't more "gas" stations realizing they are actually "filling" stations and install electric vehicle (EV) charging ports?

  There will be great disruption unless the station owners move quickly. As an EV driver, I'd much rather stop and charge at a Chili's or a Red Lobster than a gas station (because I'm going to be there for 20 to 30 minutes at least). Shopping malls and grocery stores have already figured this out and so have hotels who are busy installing chargers.

  Surprisingly, Tesla hasn't, as to date only one of its superchargers includes a shop and a place to sit!

  But who should be the disruptor here? The electric power utilities of course! EVs use power, utilities sell power, but until recently they hadn't done much to get into the business.

  Regulators have blocked the way in some cases (like California), but smart utilities, such as Green Mountain Power in Vermont, have partnered with charging companies to provide infrastructure and allow GMP customers to put remote charging right on their home's power bill!

Shouldn't the power provider want products that use more of their product?

Power companies used to get it. When I was a kid, our power company gave away nice, bright, high-power light bulbs to any customer who wanted them, and why not; they caused us to consume more electricity!

- Hotels

Will self-driving cars affect hotel stays? Well, millions sleep on airplanes as they travel from city to city; why not in cars? Perhaps they will cut out overnight stays for salespeople, change the use of hotels for short vacations.

- Healthcare

The number three reason for emergency room visits is car accidents. Almost 90% of car accidents are due to driver error, not mechanical failure, so we should expect significant changes.

Safer self-driving cars (see above) should decrease this number and change demand and design. Think about the effect on police departments, fire departments, tow trucks, insurance companies, and of course, hospitals (both emergency and long-term care) if there were fewer car accidents. Oh, and let's not forget ambulance-chasing lawyers either!

- Advertising

There are an estimated 750,000 roadside billboards in the US generating a large part of the $7 billion of annual revenue of the outdoor advertising industry. How will this change when no one is looking out the window?

Will self-driving cars move all passenger focus inside? Today it is common to see two kids in the backseat glued to their iPads watching a movie. Will this happen to the driver as well? Why not? We already know that even those who <u>are</u> driving feel compelled to look at their phones!

- Traffic Tickets

  New York City collected over $560 million in traffic fines in a recent year. If self-driving cars are (as expected) as law abiding as your grandma, what happens to that revenue and what happens to the government agencies dependent on that income?

  And if I've sent my car home by itself, and it is in a wreck, who gets arrested and who (see above) is liable?

This list could go on to include: traffic lights, auto parts stores, car washes, DUI lawyers, wreckers, bump shops, car-chase helicopters, and on and on.

Of course, the greatest impact could be on car ownership itself!

Ride sharing has already had an impact. In 1983, 87% of 19-year-olds had their license. The number was only 60% as of 2014. The number of 16-year-old license holders plummeted from 45% to 24% in a recent AAA study. Most teens say they can get wherever they want with Uber or public transit, or they can simply stay home and text each other!

Even car rental agencies are suffering with 56% of former renters giving up renting between 2016 and 2018 due to ride sharing.

If fleets of self-driving cars are available at reasonable rates, predictions are that car ownership might plummet.

The point of the outline above is not that all of these changes *will* happen with self-driving EVs – it is that they *very well might.* The point is that just *one* change will dramatically affect a broad swath of the fabric of many other businesses.

Think about it. Twenty percent of the Fortune 500 are digital companies that didn't exist 15 years ago. Which is perhaps why 70% of the CEOs of Fortune 500 companies state that their company today is a "tech company." (If they aren't, they aren't "cool!")

As a hopefully realistic futurist, my goal for this book is to outline the most impactful technologies, to open your mind to how they are being applied, and to offer ways they could be applied even more effectively in the future.

Your task (with your deep understanding of *your* industry) is to imagine how these different technologies might affect your company.

Frankly, I hope you emerge from the first half of this book just a little nervous, which serves the purpose of moving you out of "digital denial."

The second part will discuss how you can prepare and not become the next Nokia or Kodak.

IT PHASE I – SYSTEMS OF RECORD

"I think there is a world market for perhaps five computers."

—Tom Watson, Founder, IBM

When I began my business career, almost fifty years ago, the average company didn't have a computer. Believe it or not, as a travel agent I made my very first reservation by *telegram!*

Yes, our agency had a little fax-like machine that took a typewritten form, scanned it, and sent it to the local Western Union office where it was transcribed into a telegram and sent on its way. Replies came into the same machine, which "burned" the message into special paper producing considerable smoke and a barely legible message.

Most of my audiences are amazed by this story, as they should be. I will admit to being amazed myself when I saw the machine. I'd seen telegrams in movies about the "Old West" but never expected to send one.

I suspect I felt much the same as a 20-year-old does today when she joins her first company, sets down her iPhone, and stares bemused at the "green screen" computer in front of her. (You still see them at car dealers). She is probably thinking, "Did I just go through a time machine?"

My boss was a Luddite and refused to even consider upgrading to a Teletype (a typewriter-like communicator introduced in the 1930s and in widespread use in business at the time) and a computer was completely out of the question.

Few medium and small businesses had access to computing power, and if they did, they utilized "timesharing" (an early form of cloud computing) where a dial up terminal accessed a central computer for brief periods to perform accounting tasks. (My second travel agency used timesharing to produce tickets and do the books.)

This was "IT Phase One." It was a period when computers were large, centrally located, and used to make reservations, keep the books, or add up sales. They were "systems of record."

It is useful to be reminded that in those days computers cost about 8000 times more than they do today and were literally the size of a small garage.

I was once an expert witness in a 2007 lawsuit that had its beginnings in the 1980s. I had to testify about how physically large mainframe computers were in the 80s and how many programmers it took to make a change.

We had a tough time getting the jury to believe our stories as by that time many had PCs, used Excel, and had seen the iPhone introduced that year. They found my stories of past computers simply unbelievable.

The key change that moved computing forward was connecting them, which jumpstarted the evolution of computer networks.

Up until then, much of business computing involved using remote terminals with low-speed phone lines and private networks to distribute the computing power.

Ever watched an airline reservation agent (at an airport) and wondered about those cryptic entry codes typed on green screens without fill-in formats?

Systems were designed that way for a specific reason; computers were expensive and people were cheap! The idea was to make things easy for the computer and the network.

Here's what I mean. Your airline reservation number (XLTYSZ) is actually (when decoded by the computer) the physical disk address of your booking.

When the agent asked for your number (rather than your name), it made it easy for the computer to instantly find your reservation by going right to the spot on the disk where it was located!

Entries were also cryptic and all UPPERCASE to relieve the load on very slow communications lines. Today uppercase online is shouting; back then it was to reduce the complexity of transmission.

It took many weeks to train operators on these cryptic codes, but keeping things cryptic made the computer quick.

Thus, the limiting factors at the time were the expense of computing (which required it to be centralized and shared) and the low speed and expense of communications, which limited distribution of access.

What moved us to Phase II? Something you use on average three hours per day (and it isn't your phone).

IT PHASE II – SYSTEMS OF ENGAGEMENT

"So how come my local mall handles more business
in an afternoon than the Internet handles in a month?"

—Clifford Stohl for Newsweek 1995

The change that put rocket fuel in the digital revolution was, of course, the Internet.

Did you know the underlying communications design of the Internet sprang from an idea on how to protect networks during a potential nuclear war? The premise was that if one route was blocked, information would bounce around until it found its way to a final destination. Broken wires wouldn't result in lost messages.

Even though it was originally designed for communication reliability during a nuclear war, it ended up having a much different effect.

As the Internet grew, information escaped; it found its freedom. Today information is available to us all the time and we take finding an answer in a second as normal.

With all the world's information in our pockets, we tend to forget (and the younger among us never knew) a time when Internet communication was slow, unreliable, and mostly *one way.*

When I first started using the Internet in earnest (in 1996), there were no search engines. You had to know the URL of the site you wanted, type it in, and get a very limited amount of information back.

That's why the initial pages of Yahoo looked like this:

(Note – no search box!)

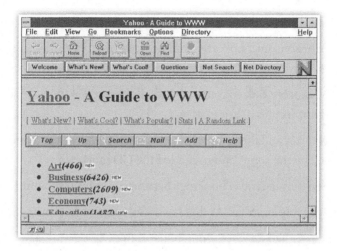

There was another reason for that paucity of design. The Internet was slow, really slow. When we started Travelocity, most home communication was at 1200 baud, compared to today's 100 megabit connections, 1200 baud = about 0.0012 megabits per second (mbps).

Yet even at that slow speed it was useful, and what made it useful was Marc Andreessen's (and others') wonderful invention of the browser. And yes, the funding for the browser was provided by the Federal Government in a bill sponsored by Al Gore, so in a way he did "invent the Internet!"

While graphical user interfaces had been around since the late 80s and the increasing power of PCs made consumer computing easier, it was the browser that unlocked the informational goldmine of the Internet.

So, why the history lesson when chances are you're familiar with the above?

Because, even though the early Internet was poorly designed, unreliable, and frustrating, it changed the game because it represented an opportunity to connect directly with customers and disrupt the competition.

For the first time, consumers could directly interact with sellers via the computer rather than face to face or via the telephone. And that set up a ripple effect of disruption.

Here are just five of the hundreds of companies that dramatically changed their industry because they leveraged the early Internet to their advantage:

- MapQuest caused maps to go digital then free.
- Amazon put book sales online, then digitized them, and now millions of them are almost free.
- Microsoft took encyclopedias digital, then Wikipedia made them free.
- Napster and then Apple took the music from "by the album" to "by the song" and imploded the CD market.
- Self-service travel bookings became an online tsunami.

To paraphrase Marc Andreessen, "Software began eating the world."

Then we had another seminal disruption.

Increasing speed allowed Internet communication to become a two-way street and we had the invention of user-generated content (UGC).

While many websites were taking print content and throwing it up on the web (with little thought about how the web was different), others had the brilliant idea to source information from the user. Consumers began writing, selling, and rating.

- Craigslist took on the Yellow Pages.
- Angie's List created an entirely new category combining the Yellow Pages and a neighbor's advice.
- eBay took on the classifieds.
- TripAdvisor took on the travel agent and guide books.
- Wikipedia took on Encyclopedia Britannica and Microsoft.

This two-way world also created the world of social media and the world's largest website (and advertising powerhouse) Facebook, which stole almost $40 billion in ad revenue from traditional media during a period when total ad spending grew only 3%.

The lack of a specific way to find what you were looking for on the Internet spawned innovation, first with Yahoo!, which used hand-curated indexes to point the way to information. Then, Google used high-power algorithms to index the web so you could search through the millions of sites being spawned every single day to find exactly what you were looking for.

Much has been written about how Google started without a business plan or business model. And it wasn't until 2000 that they started their phenomenally successful paid-search model (an invention of good friend Bill Gross from IdeaLab).

In less than 20 years, that invention now creates $100+ billion in annual advertising revenue. In fact, Google has 45% of all digital ad revenue. To put this in perspective, total digital ads are now larger than TV ads.

Think for a minute about how Google has disrupted other businesses.

Google now has garnered

- 75% of the mobile operating system market share with Android and has made $22 BILLION in profit by giving away what Microsoft was trying to sell. Steve Ballmer famously said, "Free isn't a business model." No, it isn't, unless you get your money another way, like advertising!

  Microsoft spent $8 billion to buy Nokia to try and revive its Windows phone market share, but eventually wrote it off and now has disappeared from the mobile operating system market. Gates recently said that losing to Android was, "his greatest mistake ever"[2]

- 1.5 BILLION Gmail users, and until 2017 read users emails to personalize ads and create more ad revenue [3]

- 1.3 billion videos and $3 billion in ad revenue via YouTube which is now the world's second largest search engine. Millennials spend twice the time on social video (YouTube, Facebook, and Twitter) than on TV.

The two-way Internet and UGC led to "the sharing economy" and new types of business disruption.

- Airbnb – where users turn their home or room into a profit center. Did you know Airbnb has become the world's largest hotel chain?

- Uber – where drivers turn their car into a profit center which has helped Uber become the world's largest limo company.

- LinkedIn – which began as a business-networking site. However, did you know it now gets the majority of its revenue from its recruiting business? Your bio is their resource.

- Yelp – which combined local listings and your opinion to become the go-to resource for recommendations on everything from who has the best burrito to who is the most trusted dentist or veterinarian in your area. This service earned them a billion dollars in the process.

All these "sharing" businesses use the OPA model, *"Other People's aassets."*

Airbnb's assets are your spare rooms. LinkedIn's assets are millions of CVs. eBay's assets are your used sports equipment, collectibles, and vintage clothes. YouTube's assets are your monetized videos. In each case, you or your stuff are their assets.

All of this came about because of the two-way Internet. We'll delve into how to leverage OPA in your company in the second half of the book. But first, it's time to delve into another game-changing technical innovation.

As Dean Kamen, the inventor of the Segway said, "Every once in a while, a new technology, an old problem, and a big idea turn into an innovation."

You're about to discover how you can address old problems with a new technology to create a new innovation.

MOBILE DISRUPTION

"When the iPhone came out every CIO in America said,
'You're not bringing that into my environment,' my CIO included."

—Randall Stephenson, CEO, ATT

So, what is another technical innovation that set the stage for large-scale disruption?

Mobile computing.

Consider these impressive numbers.

There are 5 billion mobile phones in the world as of this writing.

By 2020, 75% of the world's population will be connected via mobile.

If you include tablets and other mobile devices, there are 3.4 billion mobile Internet users worldwide.

A surprising fact is that mobile phone growth has outpaced the Internet's growth – even though their growth curve took off about the same time. It's hard to remember that smartphone growth didn't really take off until the iPhone was launched in 2007.

To put this in perspective, when Travelocity started in 1995, guess how we informed users of flight delays? By sending messages to pagers! There simply weren't enough message-capable mobile phones at the time.

Phones were still mostly "dumb" till Apple came along and upped the game – from dumb phones used primarily to make and receive calls to data creators.

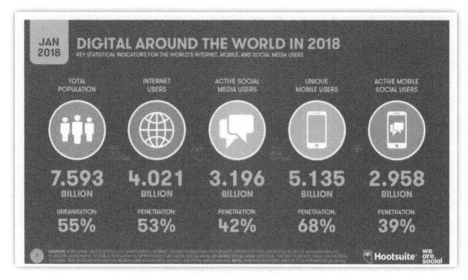

Today mobile users consume and create data at the rate of 8 exabytes yearly. They send 21 billion text messages and snap 1 trillion photos per year.

Smartphones have been *both* a business *disruptor* and a business *creator.*

The smartphone devastated the MP3 player market (sales down 90%) and the digital camera market (down 80%).

My brother is a retired National Geographic photographer. For years he trekked the world festooned with cameras, lenses, and tripods. He's still snapping magnificent photos daily, but now in an entirely new way. Recently we took a three-day train trip together. I noticed he wasn't hauling his normal gear and asked, "Where is your camera?"

He just smiled and held up his phone.

Dewitt told me he still enjoys his "big boy" cameras but he also likes the "instant gratification" of the iPhone. Its fun-to-use editing apps let him take, enhance, and experiment with photos in real time.

The postproduction software in "everyday" smartphones is now so good, it's the equivalent of a portable photo lab. In fact, Dewitt's iPhone photos are every bit as publishable as those taken with more expensive professional cameras.

Which leads us to an interesting disruption.

The trillion photos taken annually needed to be stored and shared. When I was a kid, my family was regularly invited to friends' homes to see "their vacation photos." This was usually quite a production. They would send the invitation out a few weeks in advance because they had to drop off their rolls of film off at a drug store and have it developed. Back in those days, you didn't know how your pictures turned out until you picked them up and paid for them. Sometimes, only a few were usable and worth showing or sharing. The rest got thrown away because they were blurry or you had your thumb over the lens, or something. An expensive process.

Now, photo-taking and making is free. No more trips to the drugstore. Your pictures are available the second you take them. If you don't like them, you erase them and try again. If you do like them, you share them with the world on Facebook, instantly, and even more often on Instagram.

As Carrie Fisher said, "Instant gratification just takes too long."

Instagram started as a photo-sharing site; however, it has become a disruptor in a way no one (even they) imagined.

It garnered one million users in its *first two months*. Then, just two years after it was launched, it was sold to Facebook. When purchased, Instagram had no revenue model. Repeat. It had no revenue model.

What they had, of course, were users. Over 30 million of them, which provided a wide open path to revenue. Facebook needed more mobile users and a better platform. And with their imminent IPO, they had many billions to play with, so they essentially bought Instagram to acquire its users. More instant gratification.

Today with its one billion users and 40 billion images, Instagram generates about $8 billion in ad revenue for Facebook. It owns the brand-new category of influencer marketing, where celebrities are paid to post and thereby promote products. Almost 75% of advertisers now buy influencer ads, taking revenue from print and TV and growing faster than other types of digital ads. Talk about a ripple effect of disruption.

As we learned in our self-driving car example, disruption can come right out of left field.

Others looked at the smartphone as a computing platform. Marveling at the fact that it contains not only a phone but an accelerometer, GPS, voice recorder, music player, gyroscope, light sensor, compass, and more, they set out to see how they could morph and leverage the device into even more applications.

Consider the disruption that smartphones have caused in the medical field. There are now attachments to the iPhone that make it a:

- Glucose meter
- EKG reader
- Allergen detector
- Otoscope (hearing)
- Microscope
- Breathalyzer
- Blood pressure reader

The other day I went to see my doctor to investigate a pain in my hip. Expecting to be sent for an X-ray or sonogram, I was pleasantly surprised when he reached into his pocket and pulled out a device the size of an electric shaver and plugged it into his phone. "It's a sonogram," he said. "Not quite as good as the $50,000 models but quite good enough for much of my work." We stared together at the screen on his phone, and in a few minutes, he had the problem diagnosed and we were on a way to a cure!

The "Butterfly IQ" as it is known is not just less expensive than traditional sonograms at $2,000, but by putting the technology on a chip it also eliminates multiple sonogram probes. It can perform 19 different clinical applications *and is collaborative as the sonograms can be quickly shared with doctors nearby or across the planet.* "Bones" from Star Trek has just about arrived on the scene.

The combination of the hardware with software and the computing power of the phone can create impressive disruption.

There are phone-connected glucose meters that can alert you if your kid's blood sugar spikes, and thermometers that connect with doctors on demand. There are even devices that sell your data for advertising. The Kinsa smart thermometer company segmented their customers' temperature data by ZIP Code and licensed it to Clorox as Clorox figured that sick people in those ZIP Codes would benefit from their disinfecting wipes. Wow!

Heavy industry is not far behind with add-ons like thermal imaging sensors, bar code and RFID scanners, water and gas testers, and airflow meters.

Again the disruption is that for the first time these devices reach the cloud in real time and provide not only a readout but *analysis of what the readout means.*

The iPhone created an app marketplace with the App Store and earned over $100 billion in sales. The app economy created immense, new businesses. The market cap of some app-only businesses is staggering: Uber, $70 billion? and Spotify, $30 billion?.

A side note: It's easy to become a little inured to the word "billions" these days. We hear it, see it (and read it in this book!) so often, it loses its power to impress us.

As Senator Everett Dirksen famously put it when discussing the defense budget, "A billion here, a billion there, pretty soon you're talking big money!"

Other than government spending, billions in business are a fairly new phenomenon.

Google was the first company to reach a billion users and that was just in 2011.

It used to take a super-startup seven years to reach a billion-dollar valuation. BIRD, the scooter, just did it in slightly over one!

This is a testament to how quickly digital companies can scale. Investors are betting big on the power of digital disruption to change all of commerce, and they are being rewarded by the markets.

Creative app companies realized that they could create business models based around the mobility of phone customers.

- Uber – taxi medallion prices have cratered and traditional cab rides are down dramatically worldwide. At the same time, Uber is now providing 15 million trips per day worldwide.

- Hotel Tonight – gives hotels a way to release last-minute inventory and guests a way to get a great deal for tonight. It sold to Airbnb for $400 million.

- Square – used in 250,000 businesses to accept payments via mobile. They charge less than traditional card processors, and pop-up businesses from swap meets to panhandlers have a way to accept payments.

- Venmo – who solved the problem of sharing digital money (like splitting the dinner check) has over 30 million users and transferred over $17 billion in payments in 2017.

These companies have grown so quickly that traditional business just can't keep up. When my daughter applied for a mortgage, her banker (looking at her statements) said, "Who is this Venmo guy and why do you keep sending and receiving money from him?" My daughter laughed and explained that she and her brand-new husband hadn't consolidated their accounts and were jointly paying for things with "Mr. Venmo."

To keep up with mobile disruption, companies have had to rethink their web strategy.

At Kayak we thought mobile customers would use our app to obtain "the next flight out" or a "hotel for tonight."

That turned out to be totally wrong. Our customers used our mobile product just like the desktop. The team had to throw out the old and design something new. The nice part was with a board of experienced VCs and Internet hands there wasn't any griping; instead we celebrated what we'd learned.

If we hadn't listened, and if we didn't have short feedback loops that allowed us to quickly redesign, Kayak wouldn't have over 60 million app downloads today.

Similarly, Facebook, which had only twelve mobile programmers in 2012, found by 2019 that over 900 million of its users were mobile only.

The examples above prove the adage that "audience is everything."

Startups that grow through word of mouth (WOM) don't always need a killer revenue model at inception. Instagram, Facebook, Google, and others didn't have a model until they gained an audience and determined advertising was the way to go.

Waze, which sold to Google for $1 billion, for example, has 90 million users in 128 countries – but it is just beginning to monetize with location-based advertising.

While WOM growth and no revenue can be fine for a startup, it simply doesn't work for risk-averse corporations trying to avoid disruption or who are entering new markets.

Investors, for some strange reason, seem to insist that traditional companies make money while allowing startups and new models (see Amazon or Tesla) to lose money with impunity!

What's an incumbent to do? As mentioned, we'll go into detail on how you can adapt to disruption in the last half of this book. In the meantime, think about how these disruptors crafted their products:

PLATFORM:

Some thought about how the phone could be a *platform*_for existing products. For example, a thermometer that told you what a fever of 102 in a three-month-old might mean – and then connected you instantly to a doctor.

CONTEXT:

Some thought about the *context* of how the phone was being used and how it could be deployed as a platform to revolutionize an industry. Uber recognized that both the customer and supplier were mobile users and connected them to produce a new product.

Because Uber's service is, at its core, identical to a taxi or limo, their differentiation is ease of use and user interface. A $70-billion-dollar company that is basically UI!

How could your company use platforms or context to disrupt your market?

Does your product throw off enough information that others could code apps to you? Withings scales and Fitbits data streams have spawned dozens of apps that consolidate and analyze health data, making both product and app more useful.

Or could you be the collector of information for the industry and sell it back to them as we did at SABRE?

Final note: I'd be remiss if I didn't comment on the way cell phones changed the way every phone call starts.

My parents always answered the phone with, "Hello, how are you?"

My kids with, "Whazzup, where are you?"

You see we used to know where you were. You were where the number we called was: your office or your home. Today, we have no idea.

Mobility has changed communications forever, and for better or for worse, we are now never out of touch.

But remember too that these "phones" are actually powerful computers constantly consuming and creating data.

And that is going to happen faster in the world of 5G.

SPEED KILLS – 5G

"Life's picking up speed"

—Jeff Bridges, Actor

I was a history major in college and have always loved Roman History. The Romans had measurements for distance, weight, time, and volume and more. I was surprised to read that they had no measure for speed. But in their time, it simply wasn't necessary as you moved only at the speed of foot, horse, or ship.

Today, many organizations are obsessed with speed. For good reason.

We learned at Travelocity and Kayak that the faster we made our systems, the more people purchased.

On the flipside of that, a recent study shows that every second of delay costs 7% in buyer conversion.

So, speed either wins you customers or loses you customers.

As browser tools improved loading, we turned more shoppers into buyers. The ability to include images and video dramatically increased conversion as well. (Remember, the early Internet had no video.)

What will happen with the introduction of 5G, which is 20 times faster than our current 4G cellular networks?

5G has several attributes that make it far superior to 4G.

- <u>Speed</u> – peak data rate of 20 GB (20× 4G)

- Latency – 1 millisecond latency (up to 120 times better than 4G)

- Density – 1,000,000 devices per square kilometer vs. 100,000 with 4G

- Mobility – can communicate with devices travelling at 500 kph vs. 300 kph with 4G

- Reliability – much higher than 4G

- Low Energy – very low power consumption, perhaps as much as 90% less than 4G

So, what are the practical business effects of these attributes?

"5G is like having fiber in your pocket," said John Godfrey, SVP of Samsung.

If your mobile device can communicate at 20× its current speed, what might that change?

Here are some examples:

- High-speed trains are approaching 500 kph and customers demand cell service wherever they are. 5G will ensure our transportation won't outrun our communication.

- The high speed and low latency of 5G will allow self-driving cars to communicate with each other and reduce traffic jams. Carnegie Mellon estimates it could eliminate traffic lights and reduce commute times by 60%.

- Drones need to communicate quickly with each other and with air traffic control if their promise is going to be realized.

- No need to run fiber to your home to get superfast Internet. 5G can beam it to a small antenna on your roof.

These high speeds and low latency may also create "The Internet of Skills" (IOS). IOS means that no matter what your skill, you can practice it remotely using high-speed connectivity. (BTW "latency" means the time delay before transmission starts.)

At this year's Mobile World Congress in Barcelona, there was a demonstration of this in the medical field. Surgeons three miles apart collaborated on an operation using 5G to ensure that their efforts were instantly coordinated. As 5G networks proliferate, you can imagine the benefits to healthcare personnel and patients.

Similar experiments are ongoing in industries where technicians are using high-speed video to diagnose machine failures and walk local techs through repairs. 5G will be key here to operate augmented reality glasses in real time.

At Boingo Wireless, where I'm a board member, we are looking forward to deploying 5G in the Army, Air Force, and Marine bases where we today provide Wi-Fi. (Armed Forces members, it turns out, play LOTS of video games and have "the need for speed.") It will also be key in the stadiums we power where there is real demand for higher speed mobile video and the promise of augmented reality for fans.

Of all the technologies this book discusses, the disruptions of 5G are the least defined. It is likely they will emerge as the technology is rolled out and developers can experiment, fail, and experiment again.

- If your products include mobile, how could 5G's speed allow you to change what you can do for your customers?

- Could the density and low power usage allow you to begin thinking about Internet of Things (IOT) devices in your factories to improve reliability and reduce cost?

- What could 10 gig speeds mean for your real-time analytics capability?

If you think back to the disruptions that the 1200 baud Internet caused, what could 20× that speed do? Keep your eye on the expansion of 5G as things will move quickly here.

As we discuss other technologies such as robotics, 3D Printing, and AI, keep in mind how much 5G will pave the way for disruption, just as dial up did in the past.

THE CLOUD

"The power of instant scale,"

—Reid Hoffman, Founder, LinkedIn

The combined effect of systems of engagement, UGC, and mobile computing has created massive amounts of data.

Today we create 2.5 *quintillion* bytes of data per day.

The question of where to put all this data happily intersected with some key technological advancements: the increase in computer processing power, communications bandwidth, and storage capacity.

While capability of all these technologies increased a thousand-fold from 1990 to 2010, their prices fell like a rock at the same time.

The need for real-time access to vast amounts of data by a distributed workforce and the ability to share computing power and storage was a main driver behind the creation of the cloud.

"The cloud" simply means that instead of housing your own computer locally, you use a shared and centralized service outsourced to someone else.

It can be simply Infrastructure as a Service (IAAS), where the outsourcer manages the hardware and you, the software.

Or Platform as a Service (PAAS) where the outsourcer also manages the operating system, middleware, and runtimes.

Or Software as a Service (SAAS) where you simply run an application suite (like HR or CRM) and the outsourcer manages all the hardware and software.

The cloud is sort of "back to the future" for me. My first startup, a travel agency, used dial up computing (only 300 baud) accessing a remote computer and applications to produce tickets, invoices, and create reports for our corporate clients.

How timesharing worked then will quickly show us how far computing has come today.

As computer time was expensive, we tried as hard as we could to limit it. We typed all our entries on a keyboard and they were stored to a cassette tape. When we were ready, we would "batch" uploaded the data to the mainframe. If accepted, the tickets began printing a few minutes later. That was the bad part.

Though slow, timesharing had some great attributes: I didn't worry about backup, capacity planning, or security. Those were all problems for the timesharing company. Best of all, I had no capital investment and paid only for the computer time I used.

The invention of the PC and client–server architecture killed off timesharing as it put computing into everyone's office or home.

This was faster and cheaper than timesharing, but it forced everyone to be a computer genius, and created all kinds of issues with security, backup, and constant upgrades (as many of us know so well).

The cloud and the invention of SAAS freed us from many of those problems. It took us back to the future, and a much better future it is.

The key elements of cloud computing are:

- The ability to deliver software as a service eliminates expensive site licenses and ensures one is always operating on the latest version of software. (See also PAAS and IAAS.)

- The fact that it is self-service and self-provisioning.

- That reliability, scalability, elasticity, and performance are all the responsibility of the provider.

Having run one of the world's largest data centers at American Airlines (and losing my hair while doing it), the ability to outsource some computing capabilities would have been very enticing.

Although I would have still been ultimately responsible for the uptime of all the systems, I would not have had to worry about all those issues listed above. The constant upgrades of a system that large, while attempting to never have downtime, is literally like changing the wheels on a moving car. SAAS gives that problem to someone else.

The elastic ability of the cloud to handle traffic peaks is a great feature and saves large capital dollars (particularly for startups). At Travelocity we had no idea of the avalanche of bookings we would receive during the New Year's week after our launch. It seems that everyone used the Christmas holiday to get online, dream about, and book their next vacation. Who knew?

There was no way to quickly scale our infrastructure and our crashing systems drove lots of traffic to just-launched Expedia. The cloud can make that problem go away.

Today companies are still using client–server, but now the client can be just a browser and the server can have almost unlimited capacity. When quantum computers (the next big leap) go mainstream, you can be assured that your company won't have one; it will simply access that power in the cloud as needed.

What are the most disruptive aspects of the cloud?

1. Learning

    The amount of almost instantaneous learning developers get from being directly connected with the user.

    Satya Nadella, CEO of Microsoft, found this out when he took over their server business. He bemoaned that "they lacked the feedback loop that comes from running an at scale cloud business," which his team at Bing had used to success.[4]

2. Speed of release and improvement

The ability to immediately update software to deal with bugs, competition, and add new features is a key advantage of the cloud.

For example, after one of its cars caught fire after a crash, Tesla determined that the car had hit a piece of steel scrap left on the road, which pierced the battery case.

Teslas automatically lower at speed to reduce drag. However, using the car's ability to upgrade its software over Wi-Fi, Tesla raised *all their cars* a bit to decrease the chance of this happening again. As a result, they avoided the type of recall that Chrysler recently had for a software problem that involved over 1.4 million vehicles.

Multiply that type of expedited improvement and you can imagine the problems solved, the issues averted, the money (and lives) saved.

3. No capital – pay as you go

This is computing with a credit card. The low entry cost of cloud computing is the reason two guys and a dog in Silicon Valley can have all the computing power of a Fortune 500 company.

My son's startup built an incredible video game with a team of four. Their ability to collaborate, develop, and publish via the cloud was critical to their business.

When working at Electronic Arts, he worked on games that cost hundreds of millions of dollars. Using the cloud (and many other tools), his team created a game for $350,000. Their computing costs were minimal.

The cloud's largest disruptions certainly have been in the software business. Salesforce is the quintessential example, as it used the cloud (among other things) to topple Siebel Systems, the previous market leader. Salesforce gobbled up 19% of the CRM market and now has a market cap of $155 billion.

HR software has also been transformed by the cloud. Dave Duffield founded PeopleSoft in 1987 and it was sold to Oracle in 2004 for $10 billion. Duffield immediately founded an HR cloud company, Workday, and by 2018 its market cap had reached $40 billion.

When the cloud was introduced, many CIOs at the meetings I attended were reluctant to convert their internal systems to the cloud. They worried about security issues and loss of control. But as the cloud grew and companies like Netflix, Dow Jones, and even NASA moved, those CIOs, who were under intense pressure to reduce costs, saw the light and adopted this new model.

It probably took five years, but CIOs at similar meetings are how looking for new ways to use the cloud, promoting hybrid clouds (that combine public and private clouds) and realizing it just isn't important anymore to host their applications in their own datacenter.

As Nicholas Carr, former executive editor of the *Harvard Business Review*, put it, "Utility computing will have the economic and social impacts as profound as when companies stopped generating their own power with steam engines and plugged into the newly build electric grid."

Marc Benioff strikes a similar theme in his book, *Beyond the Cloud*. After working at Oracle for years and watching companies struggle to implement enterprise software packages, he had an epiphany after watching what Amazon had done for consumers:

"I thought it could change the landscape for businesses, too … Rather than selling multimillion-dollar CD-ROM software packages that took six to eighteen months to install and required hefty investments in hardware and networking, we could sell Software as a Service … and those services could be delivered to people immediately via the Internet in the cloud."[5]

So, back to you. Time to start thinking how what you've just read could be adapted to your industry or company.

- How could a cloud-based business model and product change your business?

- If your business is becoming a "tech business," you will almost automatically *use* the cloud. The question is, how, when, and where?

- How can real-time access to big data and massive computing power change your game?

Even the most traditional of companies are utilizing cloud technology. John Deere is now selling cloud-connected tractors. GE is selling
cloud-connected jet engines.

So, we've reviewed how "The Cloud" has sped up and expanded the
ripple effect of disruption. What's next?

THE INTERNET OF THINGS

"The only danger is not to evolve."

—Jeff Bezos CEO Amazon

Remember when you first heard Captain Kirk of *Star Trek* say, "Computer, what do the sensors say about the temperature of that planet?" It certainly seemed a plausible thing to ask a computer in a science fiction drama, but pretty impossible for any of us watching the show at that time. Yet today you can ask Alexa for the temperature of your house. That is because you now have a smart sensor (thermostat) that communicates over a network without human intervention. That sensor is an Internet of Things (IOT) device.

IOT devices don't have keyboards and don't require us to ask them questions. They can sense and act on their own without any direction from us.

To make IOT more understandable, just think about smart homes, because that's where many of us interact with IOT every day. If you walk through your home, you'll encounter IOT everywhere!

My residence is about twenty-five years old and was considered a "smart home" in its day. It's pretty basic by today's standards, but it does boast lighting scenes and a sophisticated music system. But the main brain of the system is an aging MS-DOS-based processor, and now there is only one guy in town who can update it!

I purchased my vacation home five years ago and installed the most cutting-edge systems I could get at the time. I automated my drapes, lights, garage door, security system, thermostat, doorbell cam, music, leak sensors, and more. It required pulling lots of wires, a hulking server in a closet, and control pads in each room.

Now I control it all with Amazon Alexa.

If I was to buy another home today, I suspect I could do almost everything I did five years ago without wires and without hiring an installer.

If you are like most people today, your home has a burgeoning collection of connected devices – probably some that work together and the rest constitute an electronic tower of babble that require you to learn the quirks of each. That's about to change as more and more of these devices connect to each other (and you) seamlessly.

The appeal of smart building is already disrupting the construction space. "Smart" has quickly gone from "nice to have" to table stakes.

Builders are realizing that "dumb" isn't attractive to buyers. Boingo has moved from just Wi-Fi in airports to providing distributed cellular antenna systems in all types of buildings, to recently purchasing a company that works with builders to provide Wi-Fi and smart home products so every new building can be smart.

Multifamily housing operators have concluded that "smart" apartments can create new revenue streams, boost safety and security, and save energy.

But IOT isn't just about smart homes. I'm proud to say I'm a beneficiary of the Internet of Things!

Thirty years ago, I felt my heart missing beats and went to the doctor. He gave me a testing system that consisted of a VCR-tape-sized sensor that I was to hold to my chest when I felt something odd, and an "acoustic coupler" where I placed the device to send its results over the phone to the monitoring station.

It was clumsy, slow, difficult to use, and you had to catch it at the right time. Over some months my arrhythmia went away, until a few years ago when it returned.

Back to the doctor I went, but my, how the technology has changed.

Unlike the bulky book-sized monitors of old, this time my doctor injected a device the size of a paper clip into my chest. It continuously monitors my heart's performance. If my heart is out of parameters, it sends a message to the cloud, which informs the doctor. Rather than a hit and miss effort, this is fulltime. It even reports on incidents I could never have detected myself. Medication keeps the situation under control, but the monitor is there as an early warning device if there is a problem.

The medical field abounds in IOT, and in ways you might not expect. I recently gave my disruption speech to an association of senior living center executives.

I was amazed to find that *all* of the technologies I speak about, from drones to augmented reality, and particularly IOT, are being deployed in senior living.

Devices like gastric stimulators, insulin pumps, cochlear implants, and of course heart monitors are all being monitored centrally to give an overall patient view. Non-invasive thermal monitoring is being used to measure patient gait to determine if there is risk of falling (a key cause of injury and death for seniors).

From checking diet to activity monitoring to GPS positioning (no wandering off), these sensors are helping in an industry where demand is growing and skilled labor is hard to obtain.

In talking to the senior center leaders, it became clear that there are two demands that are pushing them to IOT.

One said, "I just can't find the people I need to do all the monitoring required. And given our cost pressures, it is nearly impossible to find staff that are sufficiently trained to perform all the services our residents require. IOT helps solve that problem."

Another executive related they really have two customers. One is the senior who is living in the facility, and the other is the family member who wants to be constantly updated on how Mom or Dad are doing. "IOT can help us have requested data at our fingertips when families reach out to us to inquire about one of their relatives."

Wearables like Fitbit and Apple Watch (which can now do an EKG) are providing $24 \times 7 \times 365$ health monitoring, which is a completely new thing.

A senior health executive told me recently, "We are going to find some interesting things [and many false positives] by monitoring people continuously. Over time, this should have very beneficial effects."

Heavy industry has been an early adopter of IOT, which reduces maintenance costs, increases output, decreases defects, and monitors the supply chain.

Refineries are placing thousands of smart devices throughout their facilities to monitor failures and throughput. Electric utilities are using smart devices to detect cable breaks and shut down power *before the cable hits the ground!*

Tool giant DeWalt is creating mesh networks on huge construction sites to underlay IOT. They are deploying trackable tools (a big problem on big sites), tracking workers and providing a digital backbone for other IOT providers.

Shippers, such as Maersk, are using IOT to provide a smart supply chain. They can accurately determine delivery dates, ensure goods are refrigerated en route, and manage empty containers to get them filled and earning revenue quickly.

The new Istanbul airport project required 400 tractors working on a 79 square kilometers job site for two years. The tractors were equipped with sensors and communications to provide location tracking, fault tracking, and remote diagnostics as they moved two billion cubic meters of dirt. "Without this type of technology, managing this type of project would be 'virtually impossible,'" said service manager Volkan Kus.[6]

For many manufacturers, having a smart product that collects usage and performance data is producing revolutionary feedback. Like the feedback that Microsoft got from the cloud, manufacturers (who used to get anecdotal feedback from the dealer) now get thousands of discrete usage data points on performance and usage, making their next iteration smarter and more customer-focused.

Until I spoke to the management team at Honeywell, I never realized that buildings consume 40% of global energy. What an opportunity. The ability to help building owners reduce their energy costs is profit waiting to happen.

And Honeywell, which has been regulating energy in buildings since Albert Butz built the "damper flapper" (an early thermostat) in 1885, is now using IOT to cut that energy monster down to size. All the devices we mentioned above for the home (lights, thermostats, etc.) are being deployed in buildings, but even more so.

Smart cameras provide better fire protection (is that a burned taco or a room on fire?), temperature and occupancy sensors embedded in lights along with smart dampers can control temperature room by room, and smart compressors can meter usage to load rather than just being ON or OFF.

As buildings become smarter, operators can move from just providing "red light on" messages (sensing) to telling the operator what happened – "compressor down in section 3" (meaning) to turning on the backup compressor and dispatching service (action). From sensing to meaning to action.

Action is a much higher value product than sensing and savvy companies are realizing that they need to *move from selling iron to selling outcomes.*

The ability to predict required downtime for maintenance and failure allowed 100-year-old Kaesar Kompressoren to move from selling air compressors to selling *air!* Yes, it's AAAS (sorry for the acronym) – Air as a Service.

Air as an outcome. Like selling light instead of bulbs or heat instead of a furnace.

There are hundreds of more examples of IOT in home, industry, and cities but I hope you get the idea. These devices are building "the intelligent edge" that can allow a business to reduce costs, improve safety, increase output, and reduce energy.

Time to digest this and consider how it applies to you and your company.

- Can your next product be a smart product?
- Can you gain valuable insights on user behavior and product lifecycles?
- Can your product become like my Tesla and delight me as it self-improves?

And don't think that if you sell an intangible product like insurance, you are exempt from IOT innovation. Progressive Insurance pioneered installation of a plugin car sensor that watches driving behavior and can lower rates for careful drivers.

No business is exempt from IOT. The good news is, you can leverage it. It all depends on your imagination and your determination to be the disruptor instead of the disrupted.

Jack Welch, former CEO of GE, said, "An organization's ability to learn and translate that learning into rapid action is the ultimate competitive edge."

Look around your organization.

Would you say you're leveraging IOT? Are you using it to create an intelligent edge – a competitive edge?

In our next chapter, we'll explore how you can better learn from and leverage big data.

BIG DATA

"Data is like a rock star, if not managed it can trash the place."

—Anonymous

The story of big data is a story about *fighting* disruption. That's because, in general, only big companies have big data. Thus, many of the examples you're about to read focus on how large companies used big data to beat out entrenched competitors or to outfox nimble startups.

When I was CIO at American Airlines/SABRE we thought we knew what "big data" was. SABRE was one of the largest data systems in the world in the 90s, and boy were we proud when we got to a "terabyte" of data (that is one trillion bytes).

We'd been growing data for years and finally hit that mark, but at a cost of over $10 MILLION dollars. The disk drives required were refrigerator sized and filled an area the size of a small house. Today, I have a terabyte disk in my laptop and carry a $40.00 Kindle sized spare in my briefcase.

So, cost and size were a problem with big data then, but there were other problems. If you asked the SABRE system, "Does Terry Jones have a reservation on flight 290 to Chicago?" it could answer in a millisecond.

However, if you asked, "Is Terry Jones on a flight to Chicago today?" it could not answer that at all! It simply wasn't designed for it.

In those days, databases worked much like a book, if you wanted to find a specific topic you needed to look in the index. If it wasn't in the index, it was difficult to find.

Many companies separated transactional and reporting systems to ease this problem. However as data grew, speed and simple access remained a problem.

There were specialized systems that used parallel processing with specialized hardware to solve the speed issue. At SABRE we installed Teradata systems in the mid-90s so we could ask more difficult questions over large datasets.

For example, one day our Chairman asked if I could find out why our $500 coffee makers (they are expensive since they have to work at 10,000 feet) were becoming dented and unusable. "We are throwing away money here, Terry, find out why."

Before Teradata and "big data," I'm not sure I could have found out why. But we dug in and had our system read through hundreds of flight attendant complaints. We discovered this only happened in certain cities and in certain months ... hot months. A clue!

By studying what was happening in those cities, we discovered that because our food delivery trucks were constantly moving from refrigerated areas to the hot tarmac, the ice bags for drinks became hard as rock. In order to break up the ice for serving, the flight attendants were using the $500 coffee pot to smash the ice! We placed a $3 hammer on each aircraft. Problem solved.

This one "search and solution" saved tens of thousands of dollars. That's just one example of how smart, strategic use of data can help increase revenue and reduce costs.

Using big data in this era was called "data mining." That was a good phrase because you needed huge machines to remove the "overburden" of unneeded data to find the wisdom you were looking for. Data at that time was (and in many cases still is) stored in data silos, or "data marts" where each department jealously guarded their data like a castle keep.

As the cost of storage fell, companies started keeping more of it around. Many companies now have data in the petabyte range (1000 terabytes) and

Google is estimated to have 15 exabytes or 15,000,000,000,000,000,000 bytes of data! That's a lot of zeros.

Unfortunately many of these "data warehouses" looked like one of those houses on a hoarder's show or a storage container on Storage Wars ... piles of unorganized and forgotten stuff.

These data types were also becoming more complex with the rise of the Internet and user-generated new content types that required storing: images, blogs, messages, video, and NOT just rows and columns of business data.

There needed to be a better way. Which is a calling card for disruption.

Enter Hadoop (named for the inventor's son's toy elephant).

Hadoop is an open-source ecosystem that contains a distributed file system (HDFS) and a processing engine (MapReduce/YARN). It doesn't demand a dedicated structure (like relational), is fault tolerant, and can use commodity hardware for cheap parallel processing.

It has moved us from data marts to data lakes, where thousands of streams of data flow into a massive store and allow us to "forget nothing." When I ran the data systems at SABRE, older data was shifted to old and slow disks and then to cassette tapes and finally to reel to reel tapes that required an operator to find and load. Their job title – "Tape Ape" in that politically incorrect era.

Now we have access to all our data all the time. This is the opportunity (and the curse) of big data. It is great to save everything, but storing everything can quickly become overwhelming.

Much of "big" data is "dark" data, digital exhaust. Dark data is data that is collected and forgotten. It is data that never becomes wisdom.

While many companies collect massive amounts of customer data, few use it well.

I've been an Executive Platinum member at American Airlines for fifteen years and always select the same seat. But I've never once been offered that seat when booking! Why not? AA has the data but not the wisdom. They're not turning their data into action.

Most hotel chains I frequent are the same. One chain thought it was using big data to help me and tried to be subtle about it. When I called to ask if they could swap their foam pillows for down ones they said, "But you like foam pillows!"

"No," I said, "Actually I don't."

The hotel employee said, "But our data says you like them!"

They had purposely put foam pillows in my room in the mistaken belief I liked them, and then argued with me when I said I didn't. A double whammy. They had the wrong data and a lack of wisdom in how they delivered it.

If you are going to use data to make someone happy, then take credit for it. The clerk should have said on check in, "We have already put those foam pillows you like in your room." (And I could have then corrected their data error.)

Unfortunately, I've discovered it is not unusual for there to be a gap in the efficient interpretation and execution of big data.

Gartner group said recently that 60% of big data projects fail, not due to technology but mostly due to "difficulty inherent in integrating with existing business processes and applications, management resistance, and internal politics."

So why do big data projects if most fail? Because the rewards for success can be hugely profitable.

For example, we had great difficulty in fighting the aforementioned problems at Travelocity, so finally I gave the responsibility for big data and CRM to the Chief Marketing Officer. He broke through the silos and created programs where we tracked every search of every customer. This allowed us to reach out at just the right moment (usually when the price fell) to connect with the customers and convince them to buy. This timely (and wise) leveraging of our big data let us stay competitive with Expedia, which had much bigger marketing budgets.

Gary Loveman, the former CEO of Caesars Entertainment, related how they used big data at a meeting I attended a few years ago. "When you win at our Casinos you love us. When you lose you hate us. And we really don't control either."

So they use big data to increase customer satisfaction. If you lose big, look for a terrific free room and complimentary show offer in your email the next week to bring you back. (Funny thing, if you win big, no offer! They figure you'll voluntarily want to come back – and soon.)

The "floor man" who used to offer free drinks and dinner has been replaced with a "loyalty card" that is really a big data tracking system to give you rewards points that keep you playing. After all, rewarded behavior is repeated.

Leveraging big data early and well can create great competitive advantage as I learned having a ringside seat to the launch of the first airline loyalty program, American's Advantage. It turned data *about* our frequent flyers into *profit* and increased *loyalty* from our customers.

Universities are using big data to improve graduation rates. Through the analysis of thousands of students, they have identified elements of success. Failing sophomore calculus is a strong predictor you won't make it all the way to get that engineering degree, so your advisor is messaged to intervene and either help you pass or convince you to change majors. As colleges fight for an increasingly small pool of candidates, improving graduation rates is a key success lever for all involved.

Most of us are aware how big data is increasing personalization in retail. Amazon's massive data store lets them make those great recommendations, e.g., "If you liked this, you may also like …" Spotify and Netflix use it to play you the perfect song and suggest the right movie.

But savvy companies can take big data beyond personalization. Netflix (who now has more subscribers than HBO) leveraged its massive database of movie choices not only to personalize recommendations but also to disrupt the way movies were produced.

By observing what millions of people watched, their cumulative data gave them the "secret sauce" to the types of movies people liked. When they entered movie production, this helped them create more hits than misses and forever changed the way plots are selected.

As Reid Hoffman, founder of LinkedIn, put it, "Netflix drove scale with code."[7]

Walgreens is using their 100-million-person customer base to power big data insights. With over 7.5 billion interactions annually, they are detecting unfilled prescriptions and nudging patients into compliance, improving health, reducing medical costs, and of course, increasing their profits.

McDonalds is facing increased pressure from smaller chains like Five Guys. So, they are using big data to improve service.

Did you know that when you are waiting in a long line at the McDonalds drive thru, the items featured on the menu change to those that can be quickly prepared? Their research shows them that shorter lines keep you at McDonald's rather than scooting over to a competitor, so they have adapted accordingly. And yes, the menu reverts to displaying the more complex and profitable items as soon as the line subsides.

Although large companies have collected most big data, startups are convincing entrenched players to share the data with impressive results.

Banking apps Penny, Mint, and Yodlee allow users to consolidate their financial information. According to users, this gives them much better information than their banks.

This caused Jamie Dimon, CEO of Chase, to exclaim, "Silicon Valley is coming!" He and other bankers are fighting to restrict access to their big data. They are worried that these new entrants will capture the 'edge' – the place where the customer interacts with their financial data – and sublimate the traditional bank brands.

I'm an advisor to a travel data company called Sojern. They began with the idea of placing targeted ads on those boarding passes we printed at home. As more and more travelers began to prefer mobile passes, they needed a new model. They convinced the airlines to give them the data on every search made by every traveler anonymized.

If a traveler was searching for flights for a family of four on June 6 to Orlando or Honolulu, they would then follow that traveler around the web with targeted ads showing the exact price for that trip. Then, when the traveler selected flights to Orlando, they could follow up a specifically targeted hotel ad for that family of four, then a car ad, then a Sea World ad, and so on. Today they are a new kind of Kayak, reaching further up the food chain to catch customers very early in their travel process, all based on finely curated data.

The rewards of big data are becoming increasingly apparent. In a 2015 GE study, 89% of companies thought that lack of big data adoption would result in loss of market share; 87% felt it would "shift the landscape of their industry" in three years.

Is your business based on data, but you don't even think about it?

Real estate is one such industry.

Think of Zillow, entering real estate by consolidating public housing data to give consumers transparent estimates on home pricing (and being much maligned by incumbents for not being exactly accurate). Today Zillow is a $1.3 billion-dollar real estate ad giant and moving into buying and selling homes based on superior data.

By the way, Zillow was founded by Rich Barton who also founded Expedia while at Microsoft. I suspect his learnings about broker businesses (think travel agents) and big data prompted him to realize the real estate game was ripe for disruption.

From huge industries like agriculture to small ones like home appraisal, big data is upending incumbents and wreaking havoc to old-fashioned business models.

But this is difficult work. Building and running massive data repositories is tough. Scaling systems so they can handle peak loads is expensive. Retaining talent and ensuring data is "clean" and actionable is an ongoing and pesky problem.

Luckily a solution has presented itself. Enter our next disruption – AI.

AI – IT PHASE III – SYSTEMS OF INSIGHT

"Just as electricity transformed almost everything 100 years ago, today I have a hard time thinking of an industry that AI won't transform in the next several years."

—Andrew Ng, Chief Scientist, Baidu

My journey with AI started with a phone call I got from an assistant to Ginny Rometty, the Chairman of IBM. "Ginny would like you to come up to the IBM HQ and see if you can help teach IBM Watson about travel."

It sounded interesting so I went.

And that was the start of a journey that led to cofounding an AI travel company.

But I'm ahead of myself.

IBM was one of the early leaders in AI (or cognitive computing as they called it).

My work with the IBM team taught me the key elements of AI, why it is such a game changer, and why it ushers in IT Phase III, Systems of Insight.

There are four keys that make AI disruptive.

1. It can *organize* unstructured data.

   As we learned earlier, big data is messy. It isn't rows and columns; it's posts, tweets, images, video, medical records and reports, and more. Buried in this morass of bits are insights that can help us personalize systems, recommend treatments, redesign processes – if only we could find them! AI is perfect for this.

2. AI systems *learn*.

   These are learning systems. They are the first systems that are worth more when they are old than when they are new, because they become learned. Each interaction, each transaction, each reaction gives the system a chance to improve, to become more usable and more valuable.

3. These systems can give *advice*.

   AI systems are doing a better and better job of distilling data into information and information into wisdom then advice. For example, IBM systems are working beside doctors, giving them advice on the best treatments for each patient.

4. AI systems *speak* and *understand* natural language.

   If you tell an AI system that you want to "travel to Italy this summer with my family" it can understand the concepts: Italy – country, summer – season, and family – related people. This is a huge breakthrough and to those of us using Siri and Alexa it seems so simple, but as you can imagine, it was very difficult to accomplish.

Systems that can organize unstructured data, learn, give advice, and speak in natural language are certainly light years ahead of the punch card behemoths I programmed in college. Here are just a few of the disruptions AI is causing that we'll dig into:

First, it is important to understand that AI is benefiting from the development of specialized chips to accelerate speed of AI output. There is an alphabet soup of chips doing the heavy lifting of AI: GPUs, TPUs, FGPAs, ASICS etc.

The enhancements provided by these new chips is why most AI processing is cloud-based or built directly into IOT at the chip level. This has sped up AI to the point new features are being added weekly.

Here are the five features – what Christopher Stancombe of Capgemini calls "the senses" – of AI I think are most important.

The five senses of AI:

- **Listen/Talk**

- **Monitor (see)**

- **Act**

- **Analyze**

- **Remember**

Not quite the traditional see, hear, taste, smell, and touch, but as we shall see below, AIs are already very good or getting close to the traditional senses and adding more.

SEE – Image Analysis

AIs now analyze images with an error rate of 4.8% while the human rate is about 5%. AI wins! How did this happen? It has a lot to do with *learning*.

In 2009, Google started its Image Net project. They gathered one billion images (probably only something Google could do quickly!) and hired 50,000 part-time workers to classify those images. Then they began by teaching their AI to identify a cat. It slowly improved over years but the end result is that now businesses all over the world perform image analysis as a key business enhancer.

Here are just a few of the innovative ways organizations are using AI's image analysis ability:

- An insurance company allows customers to simply send in a cell phone photo of damage and AIs determine the amount of the claim. Seems simple enough but could your company make the legal, organizational, and process changes to keep up with this leader?

- AIs are reading X-rays and MRIs with astounding accuracy and speed. They are producing "heat maps" to show what they've found and point doctors in the right direction, quickly. Could your hospital convince doctors and radiologists to adopt an AI buddy to help them or would their biases rule out this radical improvement?

- There are several companies combining satellites and AI image analysis to improve business outcomes. One looks at mall parking lots to predict retail sales or peers into oil tanks from above to forecast oil sales.

  TellusLabs used image analysis to predict US soybean production *with zero error.* Take that commodity, future gurus!! I lived next to a commodities broker for years and marveled as he wove together fact, rumor, and pure guesswork to put his bets down on the commodity roulette wheel. How will he react to a company that can actually predict the future?

- My AI startup, Wayblazer, analyzed millions of travel photos so we could show the right image at the right moment. When you asked for a hotel with golf, we didn't show you the lobby; we showed you the golf course. The result? More sales. That may sound obvious, but ten years ago, it simply wasn't possible to hand-curate millions of images.

- Facial Recognition – a burgeoning part of image analysis is facial recognition.

  In Dubai they now have a "recognition tunnel" so instead of asking for your passport you just saunter through the tunnel, the system reads your face, and you are on your way. (Is there a trap door if it doesn't recognize you?)

  - A life insurance company is approving life insurance applications via selfies! The AI does facial analysis to determine: is this person a smoker? Do they have heart disease? A clean image can result in approval in seconds. Rejection doesn't mean a no; it just means following the old interview path. Like the car example earlier, this requires competitors to throw out years of processes to compete.

These types of radical improvements remind me of the old saying, "Would your company approve the idea that formed your company?"

Hear and Speak – Natural Language

Almost 100 million Alexa smart speakers have been sold as of this writing. Google and Apple are selling millions more. These smart devices are just part of the explosion of natural language systems that are making it easier for computers and humans to communicate.

We've come a long way from those SABRE days I discussed earlier when errors were as terse as "IC" (item count) or my favorite RA8S (retry entry after eight seconds).

Today Alexa can chirp "I'm having trouble understanding right now," or "I'm not sure but I'm learning more every day." And we don't even have to slap that *Star Trek* badge on our chest to talk to the computer like Captain Kirk always did.

Voice is a great disruptor. And these new smart speakers are the new gatekeepers that disrupt how we shop and buy many products.

Think about how voice shopping has changed the buying experience. If you search Amazon or Google for toilet paper, you get perhaps twenty brands shown above the fold. If you ask Alexa she will say, "Amazon's choice for toilet paper is Angel Soft Bath Tissue, would you like to buy it"? Before you had twenty choices, now you have but one.

What a lock! If you think buying search terms in Google is expensive, think about where this could end up, with Amazon and Google controlling most of all recommendations!

Voice is reducing errors and increasing output all over industry. Lab workers are asking smart speakers questions and thus not having to stop, remove gloves, wash hands, and type on a keyboard. Industrial workers are asking voice AIs to assist in inspections, "How hot should that flow be?" And of course, consumers are happily chatting with cars, TVs, light fixtures, and yes, even toilets.

Voice frees customers from the constraints of text input, no more sliders, check boxes, or captchas. Starbucks' new voice app demonstrates the ability to order the most bizarre combinations as its demo shows a customer ordering a "double upside down macchiato half decaf and a splash of cream in a grande cup." Try that in a text-based app or at a drive thru.

The winners in voice will be those who quickly build large voice graphs that can understand and react to consumer input. Think of it this way. The reason you scream "Agent, Agent, Agent" to your favorite airline voice response system is not because it cannot understand the words you are saying; it just doesn't know what to do. It takes deep learning and expensive systems to turn voice commands into action.

Chat

Voice isn't the only natural language input; text is still huge and chatbots have popped up all over in both B2C and B2B. Customer support has been provided by chat for many years. If you are like me, you feel that many times chatting is faster and easier than waiting to talk to a phone rep. Today the person chatting with you is more and more likely to be an AI-based bot.

There are literally thousands of "bots" out there and like people some are stupid and some are genius. I can't say that Taco Bell's "taco bot" is an idea whose time has come and there are airline-booking bots that ask more questions than any travel agent could have thought up, resulting in a booking process that is frustrating and slow.

The best bots are disrupting service by reducing costs and increasing loyalty of customers who get quick and accurate answers. The 800 Flowers bot offers great suggestions with images if you are in a rush to get flowers for that important date that slipped your mind.

At Wayblazer we worked hard to make our bot into a new paradigm for booking travel. It was not just text-based but showed your products and images with each interaction. A conversation might go like this:

We found that chat allowed users to dream more about the potential of their vacation. If they were searching for tomorrow, the searches tended to be cut and dried, "A hotel tomorrow on Michigan Avenue in Chicago under $100.00."

But if they were searching thirty or more days out they tended to say, "I want a beach hotel in Cancun with a great golf course, fantastic pool, and activities for kids," and we could find that exact product. Try that with Travelocity, which only allows for city and date!

This new method resulted in conversion increases up to 40%!

AI is also helping the agent side of the conversation as well. I recently met with CRESTA, a company that enhances sales conversations by first analyzing all your past sales chats to see what works best. From this data it extracts the insights on exactly what to say and when to say it. By making the right suggestion at the right moment to the sales agent, they have increased sales conversion up to 25% and decreased time to agent productivity by almost 75%.

With 54% of millennials preferring chat to voice, it is sure surprising that only 54% of online retailers offer it.

As in all other examples, the size of the training database matters. That is why Google and Amazon have such a lead in speech. With over 100 million devices deployed, their conversational learning is happening at warp speed, capturing consumers and leaving others to look for niche markets (like customer service).

William Gibson, the sci-fi author said, "The future is already here – it's just not evenly distributed."

And that certainly is true in AI. According to McKinsey, 30% of financial services and hi-tech companies have adopted AI while only 14% of travel companies have. And the leaders are investing much faster than the laggards.

As early adopters take the lead in learning customer behavior and it will be hard for laggards to catch up in a constant learning environment.

You might want to check out McKinsey's report on AI adoption and see where your industry stands.

ACT –ANALYZE – REMEMBER

My good friend and business partner Manoj Saxena (who for many years was GM of IBM Watson) has an AI company that works in many industries. Cognitive Scale has built a suite of impressive AI tools helping industries from health care to finance.

His company built a wonderful app that exemplifies AI's ability to act to help kids with severe allergies. They used the power of AI to combine structured and unstructured data to inform a set of healthcare actions. By combining patient data, pollen data, air quality data, hospital data, and more, they began to look at impacts and outcomes of high pollen concentrations. They distilled lots of data into the right data, and many actions into the correct action to help patients.

Here is how it works.

- **Descriptive** – What is going to happen? Pollen count Tuesday off the charts.

- **Diagnostic** – What does that mean? 17 children at risk; 3 may have to be admitted to hospital; 2 have not filled their prescriptions.

- **Predictive** – What might happen next? Two might end up in the ER, one without insurance.

- **Prescriptive** – What is the best course of action? Inform parents and school nurse. Mail out inhalers. Send Uber to retrieve most at risk.

- **Deductive** – What did we learn? How many were affected? What action worked best?

Just think about the difference this makes for families dealing with allergies. The hard-working case agents at the hospital could never have waded through hundreds of files to ferret out these cases and help the at-risk patients. But AI learning systems can. Yet another example of how disruptive technologies aren't just making things easier, faster, cheaper and more convenient, they're saving lives.

As the new healthcare consortium of Amazon, Chase, and Berkshire Hathaway comes to fruition, are these the types of predictive programs they will use to upend the healthcare market?

This example, and the earlier one about Honeywell moving from sensing to meaning to action, show the power of AI to help companies make better decisions, take preventative action, and even create new, more effective products and services.

Combining AIs

The much discussed "self-driving car" is a wonderful example of combining almost all of AI's capabilities to achieve an outcome.

My Tesla uses sophisticated cameras and sensors to detect the world around it. By saving everything it sees and detects while I'm driving and sending that learning to the cloud, all Teslas become smarter with every software update. This data is then used to "augment" human capability to prevent potential crashes. It can "see" an accident coming and react and stop before you ever could.

While there aren't too many autonomous vehicles on the road yet, there are many OFF the road. Rio Tinto is deploying massive autonomous trucks in its mines, where they drive on a closed course with no risk to other trucks or people, and dramatically reducing costs vs. competitors.

Softbank recently invested almost a billion dollars in an AI-based robotic delivery startup company. Its small, almost cart-like, wagons will drive mostly on sidewalks at low speeds and will probably get approval to operate from many cities, while they get smarter every day. Certainly as Amazon enters the grocery market in a big way, they will adopt some automated delivery process. Is your grocery company ready?

But don't let my enthusiasm for AI lull you into thinking AI is easy; *it isn't!*

While it no longer requires your own research lab to implement, there is one barrier you need to conquer, and that's *training*.

I debated whether to include a section on training in a disruption book, but I decided it was important to do so because if you don't train your AI properly, it won't disrupt anything.

As we discussed earlier, Google spent years training its image AI to make it usable for general use. But you have to add your domain knowledge as well.

Be prepared to gather chat logs, reviews. sensor data, and the like and feed into the AI's maw. After processing, you must test, evaluate results, and improve the software just like any other computer program. Understand that "supervised training" isn't enough. You'll need to let your AI free in the wild to learn on its own.

At Wayblazer, one customer asked us to improve the relevance of their hotel images.

As we had already used AI to discover the attributes of millions of images we agreed, but added it would take natural language search to produce the kinds of questions that would allow us to provide the right images.

A search asking for tennis and fine restaurants would be the signal to provide the appropriate images. The client demurred. "No," they said, "No natural language. Just improve the image presentation."

We didn't think it would work but as a scrappy startup decided to try, and machine learning surprised us. Because the client had a huge volume of searches, the system was able to present thousands of images to customers and watch what they clicked on and make instant adjustments. (In traditional clickstream analysis, the process takes weeks or months.) Over about ninety days, the improved images converted more shoppers into buyers, a bottom-line win for the client and for us.

We had another customer who refused to let their AI out in the wild. They spent more than two years testing and retesting the product, discovering and fixing defects. While this process can work if you have enough brute force (and patience), it takes a long time.

As John Kelly, at the time Senior VP of Research at IBM, told me, "Developing Watson to play Jeopardy was an interesting process. When we finished programming, it was like a toddler, after that it was all about learning. It had to play tens of thousands of rounds of Jeopardy to eventually learn to beat the best players."

AI training is just like any other form of education: it requires iteration.

Even with all that trial and error learning, you may still not have a "wunderkind." A client called Wayblazer one day and exclaimed, "Your program is stupid, it cannot recommend the right hotel for a teenager vs. the right one for a toddler."

As we were using our software but their data, we inspected their data and discovered neither the word "toddler" nor the word "teen." We called back and explained that AI is not omniscient. If they could tell us the attributes of a "teen" hotel or a "toddler" hotel, we'd be happy to add them to the system and it would work fine. AI can't read minds. If the answer isn't in the data, no AI can find it.

Another time, we had a client complain that we were identifying a hotel as a "golf resort," and they were sure it didn't have golf. We did some research and discovered it did have golf, sort of. It actually had mini golf!

The image AI had correctly identified a photo with a golf hole and flag, but had no context that a one-foot-high flag was a tipoff to mini golf. So. you can train and train but you still need human quality control to catch the subtle inferences AI can't.

Former GM of IBM Watson, David Kenny, explained to me that he felt that the most impactful implementations of AI for business would come when companies combined public data, industry data, and corporate data in new and innovative ways.

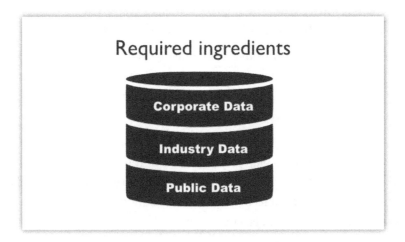

While Google, Microsoft, and Amazon will analyze public and industry data, it is the data tucked in those corporate data silos and lakes that may truly revolutionize industry. As companies use AI to enhance their products they may find, as we did at American Airlines, that their data is worth more than their current products. (For a time SABRE was worth more than American Airlines!)

Another Watson example may serve to illuminate Kenny's point. The Watson team created a product called "Chef Watson" to illustrate how data can be combined in new ways. They fed their AI thousands of recipes from *Bon Appetite,* all the food ingredients they could collect and research in "hedonic psychophysics" – the psychology of what people find pleasant. They then directed the AI to create completely new recipes and try to combine ingredients in novel amalgamations.

I got to taste a few. Some of the results were hideous, some were amazing … like "Austrian Chocolate Burritos." The point was to create something new that pushed chefs out of their comfort zone. Chefs noted they never would have thought to combine ingredients the way Watson did, which was the purpose of the experiment.

The same is true in your business. Combining data in new ways allows "systems of insight" to lead you down paths you may not have considered.

At Wayblazer, research on tens of thousands of consumer reviews discovered such paths to insights. I called it *"What are you unknown for?"*

An example I found was from Hotel du Louvre in Paris. Now with a name like that you know it will be close to the Louvre. Indeed many of the reviews lauded the quick access to the museum. But the system also produced a large number of reviews that shared how close it was to the Jardin des Tuileries, a very popular tourist destination. Yet the hotel's website did not even mention the garden, much less market it. It was an "unknown" asset waiting to be leveraged. Adding some promotional text and search keywords could generate more bookings.

Proctor and Gamble created a new franchise business, Tide Dry Cleaners, by combining consumer insights about deficits in the dry-cleaning industry, its brand, and its own insights into consumer household cleaning habits.[8]

These new franchises have a drive thru, 24-hour drop off and pickup, same-day service, and are environmentally friendly – all attributes they discovered people wanted from studying and analyzing their data.

What amazing way are customers using your product that is hidden in your data?

- Like Tide Dry Cleaners, what options do your customers want and need that they'll gladly pay for?

What new business can you create by teasing insights out of your data lake?

- Like a guy named the Amazon Whisperer. He looks for products with lots of bad reviews, and then builds a new product that eliminates those problems!

How can AI and data enhance your existing product to create a new revenue stream?

- Like Caterpillar smart diggers.

Want good news? As AI development moves forward at breakneck speed, you don't have to take this journey alone. The world's leading software companies all have products you can deploy today on your AI journey. Salesforce has Einstein, Google has TensorFlow, Microsoft has Azure, IBM has Watson.

There are also AI systems already developed for almost every industry and almost every department in your company from HR to marketing. There are also AI toolsets in NLP, visualization, text analysis, etc.

Ready to begin utilizing AI?

I'd encourage you to use Other People's Money (OPM). Find a startup that has created a trained AI for your industry and experiment with it. These VC-backed companies are hungry for a proof of concept, which means you can test at low risk and at reduced costs.

AI can produce elegant results, but training and programming it is like going to school. It takes time, dedication, and can be difficult.

But as Michelle Obama says, "Education is the one thing they can't take away from you."

AI AND YOU

"The promise of artificial intelligence and computer science vastly outweighs the impact it could have on some jobs in the same way, that, while the invention of the airplane negatively affected the railroad industry, it opened a much wide door to human progress."

—Paul Allen, Co Founder, Microsoft

Many experts are prognosticating that AI will be the most impactful technological advancement of the century (some say of all time). I'd have to agree with the first.

My work with AI has shown me so many ways it can improve products.

AI reminds me of the point of the TV ads I used to see for the chemical company BASF. They said, "We don't make the dress, we make it brighter. We don't make the carpet, we make it tougher. We don't make the sunscreen, we make it stronger."

Their point was they were a powerful additive to existing systems.

AI provides similar additive capabilities:

- Drones cannot only apply pesticides; with AI image analysis they can apply the right amount to the right weed at the right moment. Are you in the pesticide application business? Do you have your drone yet?

- AI-enhanced text analysis can move beyond keyword selection to determine the sentiment of a product review and not only separate the plaudits from the jeers but show the right review at the right moment. Does your ecommerce site do this yet?

- AI-enhanced credit analysis tools help my friend Brian Barth's company Uplift make credit decisions in seconds as the online customer's mouse is poised to decide whether to click on and buy that expensive vacation. Guess what,he's not a bank.

- AI-based baby monitors move beyond sending you the baby's cry to report changes in location, temperature, breathing, sleep, crying pattern, and more. Is your company still making baby monitors that are voice only? Watch out!

All the technologies discussed so far can be enhanced by the "six senses" of AI: vision, speech, hearing, recollection, analysis, and action.

Somewhere out there is a startup thinking about how AI can be added to your industry's products. They will either sell it to you or try to kill you with it.

Get your thinking cap on and research how AI can help open doors, make your products smarter, and accelerate your organization's progress.

DRONES

"Drones overall will be more impactful than
I think people recognize, in positive ways to help society."

—Bill Gates, Founder, Microsoft`

Many people think drones are fairly new inventions, but remotely controlled vehicles have been around a very long time. In fact, Nikola Tesla invented perhaps the first drone with a remote-controlled boat in 1898.

Military drones were used in WWI and WWII with some success. Highly sophisticated drones were used in the Afghanistan and Iraq wars.

Hobbyists have also pushed technology forward. First, they built remote control airplanes, then they used game controllers and home-brew tech to build early quad copters.

Commercial drones are another story. Like many other disruptions, they grew out of a combination of emerging technologies. Combining better batteries, advanced mapping, obstacle avoidance, tiny cameras, thermal sensing, and more has been critical to their introduction. Advanced, mostly AI-based, autopilot software allows them to fly with limited or no pilot interaction.

While the first commercial drone permit was issued in 2006, only one or two per year were issued for the next eight years. It jumped to a thousand in 2015 and has gone straight up ever since.

Agriculture was one of the first industries to capitalize on drone technology. As in many new technologies, the first creations merely substituted a robot for a person.

Drone crop dusters, for example, initially simply reduced cost. But then innovation took over and things improved quickly. Using smaller drones that fly at low altitude, DJI Drones estimates that it can cover fields 40% to 60% faster than manual spraying with significantly less waste. Thermal and AI imaging tell farmers where plants are failing, where to apply more fertilizer and more water.

Mapping drones help guide automated tractors, count plants, analyze pests, and spot disease. Drones are also monitoring animal herds with both visual and thermal sensors to ensure health and proper location.

The market for drones in agriculture is already exceeding $32 billion.

Infrastructure monitoring could be even larger, over $45 billion. Early users include power companies using drones for line inspection and monitoring.

Construction companies are observing construction sites for safety, Security, asset protection, and progress reports. Governments are checking bridges for safety.

Insurance companies have found drones an easy way to immediately enter disaster sites to inspect property and estimate losses. First responders are also sending drones into disaster areas to provide delivery of drugs and medical equipment.

Delivery drones have been seen both as a great enhancement and a buzzing problem since Amazon announced theirs.

The FAA has yet to approve commercial drone operations except on your own property or in very sparsely populated areas (like in Nevada, where I live – there simply isn't much to hit!).

But experiments are underway where drones are delivering rescue equipment to save potential drowning victims and drop life-saving equipment where rescuers simply can't go quickly or safely.

One company I feature in my presentations is Zipline, which has a lifesaving mission. I had an opportunity to meet their founder, Keller

Rinaudo, a serial entrepreneur. He told me how Zipline had discovered a novel way to bypass strict drone regulations and provide service to the community at the same time. They launched operations in Africa where at the time there were no drone prohabitions.

Zipline uses autonomous, electric aircraft to deliver blood to hospitals and medical centers on demand. These amazing drones look like airplanes, not helicopters. They fly at 80 mph and can drop their product in the space of two parking spaces.

Rinaudo (a Harvard double major in economics and biotechnology) determined that blood was the right product to begin with. Blood is a highly diverse product with limited shelf life. When it is needed, it is needed right away. They partnered with the Rwandan Department of Health, and in a country with difficult transportation infrastructure, this seemed a great solution. Less blood is stored in each hospital and *none* of the blood expires since it is delivered on demand in less than thirty minutes.

Keller told me they failed a lot in the beginning. (And here failure is literally crashing airplanes.) The catapult that launched the drones wasn't strong enough and the initial landing system (a couple of fishing poles with a rope in between to catch the plane and a Walmart "Bouncy Bounce" to cushion the fall) didn't exactly work out!

But they kept sweeping up the pieces and trying again and again.

Their aircraft fly low enough that they can use cell phones for navigation and to "de-conflict" from other Zipline drones. (Keller mentioned that that their cellphone bills are quite bizarre with all the roaming 150 daily cross-country flights produce!)

To satisfy the Rwandan FAA, they also needed to produce an interface to the traditional aircraft tracking system so the government could make sure the drones and traditional aircraft stayed far apart. They did this with an app on an iPad. Wow!

As you might imagine, other African countries are interested and Zipline has already moved into Ghana. And, surprise, surprise, they soon will launch in North Carolina.

Zipline caught the eye of Elaine Chou, the US Secretary of Transportation. The DOT began talks to see how the product could be deployed in the US.

By going to Africa first, Rinaudo was able to test his new product in a less regulated area and have enough success to get noticed by a highly regulated one.

I suspect Zipline would still be stuck on the runway if their plan had been to start by delivering pizza in New York.

Despite the naysayers of home drone delivery, just remember this one fact. According to Rinaudo, HALF of Amazon's packages are less than five pounds, just perfect for drone delivery.

While drones could decrease the number of delivery driver and tower inspector jobs, it is estimated that drone technology could actually create more than 100,000 jobs in the next decade.[9]

As with our other disruptive technologies, some applications are easy to see, like a drone crop duster, drone package delivery, or tracking criminals. Others require us to look through a new lens to see where drones might be applied to game-changing effect:

- At a recent conference I saw a drone mounted with sophisticated "sniffing" sensors patrol a hundred-acre refinery searching for methane leaks..

- Airlines have begun using drones to inspect aircraft for hail damage. Then one smart company showed up with an AI-enhanced drone that compared the last scan with the current one (using image AIs) to quickly point out dings.

- Drones at sea? Maersk is testing drone container ships, and self-sailing drones can predict weather while far out at sea.

- Experiments are being conducted with firefighting drones. Not only can they reduce potential pilot injury, they can firefight 24 × 7 as flying in the dark is no problem.

- In fact, drones are flying at night in the dark in grocery stores to look for out-of-stock items. They then send out the SOS for reorders. If your store is open 24 hours, you'd better duck at 3 a.m.!

If you move things, inspect things, grow things, advertise things, or defend things, drones are definitely coming for you and your business.

Remember disruption is about reimagining what is possible with new technology.

Case in point. Zipline started out with a simple idea. Drones could quickly deliver blood on demand to places that were difficult to reach. This reduced time and cost and saved lives. However, there were other benefits that weren't obvious at first.

- If a patient was bleeding out, they could send flight after flight and keep the patient alive. It's happened more than once as local hospitals can't store that much blood.

- If a patient with a rare blood type showed up at a remote location, they could be serviced at the site instead of having to travel to the capital city (and perhaps not make it in time).

- Because blood is difficult to collect and has a short shelf life, centralizing storage reduced both issues.

- Africans are accustomed to using cell phones for banking (M-Pesa) so ordering blood on demand this way wasn't a problem (as it might have been in the US). They send a text and have the blood in 30 minutes.

The point of all this? Don't just look to improve your product or services. Reimagine what they can do. Look for never-before-done opportunities just waiting to be discovered ... and disrupted.

Ash Maurya, creator of Lean Canvas, says, "Life's too short to build something nobody wants."

Agreed. Our next chapter shares innovative ways 3D printing can help you build things you know people want, need, and will use.

ADDITIVE MANUFACTURING – 3D PRINTING

"3D printing is going to be way bigger
than 3D companies are saying."

—Credit Suisse

3D printing, or as it is now called by many, additive manufacturing, came about by looking at an old process in a new way.

Automated milling machines are "subtractive"; they take a large chunk of metal and cut away at it to make a gear.

Physicist Chuck Hull, frustrated by how long it took to make small custom parts using milling at his company, came up with an "additive" process, called stereolithography.

Somewhat like an inkjet printer, 3D printers spray layers and layers of substrate to "additively" build up an object that is solidified with UV light. Newer printers "grow" components (rather than subtracting) using computer-aided design (CAD) files to direct a laser beam through layers of fine metal powder.

If you're still confused about how this amazingly complex process works, I suggest you take a minute to watch some YouTube videos. There are thousands and they are improving all the time, so spend a minute and check some out. For now, I'll try to do justice to this gee-whiz technology with words.

Today many 3D printed objects begin with a CAD file that an engineer has created of the desired end product. Or one might perform a 3D scan of an object that you want to copy (like a priceless Greek sculpture).

Either way the resulting file is sent to the printer which (starting from nothing) sprays a plastic-like substance (again like an inkjet printer) in tiny increments to create the final object. It is as if a sculptor, rather than starting with a block of stone that she carved into a bust, started with handfuls of marble dust and slowly created the final product.

Some people think 3D printing is a recent phenomenon and an "overnight success," but it actually started development more than 35 years ago.

In my immersion in all things disruptive, I've come to the conclusion it is one of the most powerful disruptive forces currently coming to fruition.

In 2015, GE gained FAA approval to make the first jet engine part via 3D printing: a fuel nozzle. By 2018, they had delivered 30,000 of them.

It's quite a remarkable product. It combines what was 20 parts into a single unit.

Jet Engine Fuel Nozzle

Like many manufactured parts today, I suspect its previous incarnation might have been constructed this way:

- Each of the twenty subassemblies was made in a small factory (perhaps in China) where raw materials were forged to create the finished part.

- The parts were then collected at an assembly plant and put together.

- The finished product was then stored in a warehouse.

- As it was needed it was put on a boat then a truck and shipped to GE for assembly.

Now the part can be made either on the assembly line or in a shop close by.

Think about how that changes the supply chain. The previous part required materials suppliers, sub-manufacturers, sub-assemblers, truckers, customs brokers, insurers, and container shippers, often located in different parts of the country or world. And, of course, there was the initial deal making, price negotiation, cross-border communication, and ongoing coordination required to go from ideation to production to delivery.

The new part requires *none of these companies or processes.* GE gets a part that is cheaper, lighter, and stronger, with no subparts to maintain. And it arrives faster with no inventory cost!

That's disruption!

If you add AI into the design process, you get even more exciting developments.

General Motors recently experimented with a very simple part: a seat bracket.

Like our example earlier, it was made up of eight separate parts from several manufacturers. Using Autodesk software, an advanced AI was asked to redesign the bracket for 3D printing. After generating 150 potential designs, the engineers selected one that looked quite like a Klingon warrior spaceship.

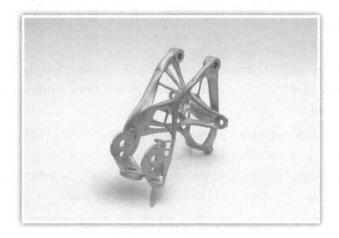

(source: GM Press Release)

Why use such a weird part? Because it is 40% lighter and 20% stronger than the previous bracket and was <u>one</u> piece.[10]

Imagine if hundreds of car parts could be made 40% lighter and 20% stronger. That's quite an impact on mileage, safety, and price.

The seat bracket was just an experiment as 3D printing is currently not fast enough to keep up with a car assembly line, yet most think that will change … and soon.

Ready for another unexpected use of 3D printing? Wait for it … hearing aids!

Today 98% of hearing aids are 3D printed according to a 2017 article by PWC.

Amazingly this changeover happened in less than 500 days.[11]

Audiologists now use laser scanning and CAD to complete a digital model of your ear and send it on to the manufacturer. There, what was previously a primarily manual process is now almost completely automated.

Customization, speed, and cost savings are driving adoption of this technology. And although the capital cost may be initially high, it's offset by the advantage of having fewer parts and no inventory.

A business colleague used to have two very clunky hearing aids. He dealt with them because they were better than nothing, but they didn't fit well or work well.

Today with 3D scanning and printing, his hearing aids would be custom-designed for <u>his</u> ear. They would fit and work much better, with less frustration.

People complain that 3D printing is a slow process, but let's put things in perspective. Remember the old story about two guys being chased by a lion? One says, "I'm not sure we can outrun a lion." The other replies, "I don't have to outrun the lion, I only have to outrun you!"

Similarly, 3D printing doesn't have to deliver parts in seconds, just significantly faster than your current method of ordering, shipping, and waiting.

Here are just a few of the industries experimenting with 3D printing:

- Prosthetics are being customized and delivered quickly.
- Clothing can be made just for you.
- Entire homes (yes, I said HOMES) have been printed in Moscow and Dubai.
- UPS is converting some hub warehouses into 3D printing factories for spare parts so they can be delivered same day.

What do you manufacture today that could be changed by this technology?

- If you make any physical product, you need to begin proto-typing using 3D printing. You can go directly from CAD to model quickly and iterate cheaply.
- If you are running low volume (like GE), perhaps you can put parts directly into production.

I want you to see 3D printing as an opportunity, not a threat. But you WILL have to change:

- If you are the parts assembler, perhaps you can open a 3D printing job shop right next to your customer and produce parts for them.

- Rather than just taking the order the way the customer specs it, perhaps you could use AI to take them back a highly improved part.

- Perhaps you can become the source for hard to find and no longer manufactured parts by custom-making them with 3D.

Use 3D printing to BE the disruptor!

VIRTUAL REALITY/ AUGMENTED REALITY = MIXED REALITY

"A new way to collaborate and communicate
where the physical and virtual worlds come together."

—Satya Nadella, CEO, Microsoft

When you think about it, virtual reality (VR) has been around forever. It's just that in the old days, when we read a book or played a text-based dungeon game, the virtual part *was in our mind.*

My mom made me a reader. Growing up, she read to me. Then, I couldn't get enough and bugged her every week to go to the library to get more books. I just loved to lose myself in the imaginary worlds that reading created.

Today's VR is of course not just in our mind. It's in our eyes. We see and are immersed in worlds created by others.

Much like video games and movies, VR software has progressed to the point it is quite difficult to know where reality leaves off and the virtual begins.

VR in industry was initially limited by cost of production and equipment costs, but today many industries are using it to enhance or create entirely new products and services. For example:

Training

Doctors at the University of Minnesota Masonic Children's Hospital use VR to help them train for a separation of co-joined twins.

By experimenting with a virtual model of the children, the doctors discovered that it would be better to flip the kids over and approach the operation from a new angle in order to succeed. "According to the physicians that simple solution may have saved the twins' lives."[12]

Doctors in Los Angeles Children's Hospital are tossing the old-fashioned plastic models that have been used for decades and using VR to practice risky or complicated procedures, saving hundreds of thousands of dollars a year.[13]

Is this disruption or just better business?

With 80% of Americans searching the Internet for health-related subjects, care providers are aggressively promoting their use of cutting-edge technology to appeal to today's more-informed consumers. Those who don't deploy are being left behind, so it looks like disruption to me.

VR training allows companies to train employees quickly and cheaply on processes that are dangerous or impossible to simulate.

For example, power companies now use virtual training to teach employees how to handle high voltage. Imagine the relief you'd feel to be able to learn this risky trade – without the risk of being electrocuted for your mistakes.

Walmart is training clerks to deal with difficult people – including those fights that sometimes breakout on Black Friday – with simulations and virtual roleplays.

When I worked at American Airlines, I'd occasionally get to take a big customer for a ride in our state-of-the-art (at the time) multimillion-dollar flight simulators. The experience was so real that some participants got airsick.

Today the Air Force is testing VR as a replacement for those expensive simulators. The reduction in overall expenses and time is dramatic. They graduated a group of students in four months from basic flight training, a process that normally takes a year. And the VR gear that replaces each million-dollar simulator is a fraction of the costs at under $50,000.[14]

Education is the largest projected market for VR. That's not surprising given the results of a new study from China.

Students were divided into two groups (VR and non-VR) and given a course in astrophysics. Ninety percent of the VR students passed the course while only 40% of the non-VR students did. Given the theoretical nature of astrophysics, the immersive nature of VR seemed to work better for these students.[15]

Given the time all kids spend today in the worlds created by video games, perhaps that result isn't surprising.

It reminds me of a story a friend told me about his interaction with his son.

He called and called his son John to come down from his room and go to school, but as usual got no reaction. Climbing up to his son's room, he found John immersed in a video game. Sporting a headset with a microphone, John was leading a team with members in four countries as they closed in on their fictitious objective. John sighed as his dad tapped him on the head and gave him the signal they had to leave right now.

His son wasn't doing well in school and my friend got to thinking about why. It jumped out at him. At home, online, John was leading an international team, coordinating plans and objectives, using cutting-edge tools to enhance problem solving, crisis communications, collaboration and feeding his endorphins by winning.

Twenty minutes later in class, he's watching his teacher read from a textbook and write on a chalkboard, using techniques that haven't changed in a hundred years.

Is it any wonder that the active, sensory engagement of VR has been proven to enhance learning and has enormous potential for application in schools?

Healthcare

Elder care facilities are experimenting with VR travel for residents. By offering "virtual tours" of far-away places they can keep residents mentally engaged. Instead of being "shut-in" and feeling "shut-down," residents can travel just about anywhere, without getting out of their chair.

Doctors have also been testing VR as a pain reliever. By diverting a patient's mind in a virtual world, they forget about their intractable pain!

I was recently in Iceland for the U.S. Dept. of State working with startups. I did one-on-one sessions with almost thirty and one was a VR startup. It particularly caught my eye as it focused on meditation through VR views of the wilderness. As I am Chairman of a large girls and boys wilderness camp, and have seen first hand the calming effect of being in the woods, I had to try it.

It worked!

Ask yourself:

1. What tasks are dangerous or risky for our employees to learn?

2. What "live operations" are very expensive to train?

3. What procedures could be simulated and learned more quickly?

4. How could a competitor disrupt my business by deploying VR?

Remember my example of the cryptic language that SABRE required because "computers were expensive and people were cheap?"

That scenario is now flipped. Using VR for training radically reduces time for new employees to become productive and significantly reduces errors in repairing complex machines. Now "technology is cheap and people are expensive!"

VR not only reduces time, money, and risk, you can use it to your advantage to improve the services you provide for customers *and* employees and disrupt those who don't.

AUGMENTED REALITY (AR)

"Simply put ... augmented reality will change the way
you work, play, connect and learn."

—Tim Cook, CEO, Apple

Augmented reality (AR) superimposes a computer-generated image on a
user's view of the real world, creating a composite view.

Here is a travel example –

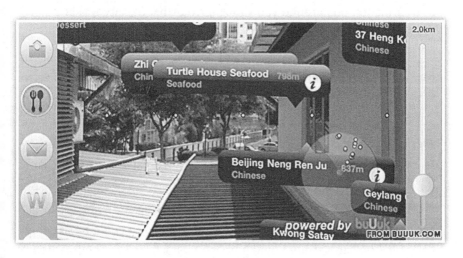

In the short term, AR is moving faster in business than VR.

Most of us recall Google Glass and other AR experiments. These systems, while interesting, were either too early, which meant poor quality, or too expensive. However, in industry, the benefits of AR are worth the investment for many.

Today, workers don a pair of AR glasses to expedite their training. If a worker needs to perform a complex task they rarely need to tackle, AR can show them the way, highlighting the part of the machine they need to replace, and showing them the right tool to use.

AR in construction can quickly point out the "as built" vs. "plan" to architects and resolve problems quickly.

As AR begins to be built into phones, retailers are using it to allow customers to perform what I call "seemagining" what a product will look like in use.

Furniture companies are allowing you to place that chair right where it will go in your home. Art dealers are letting you place the painting on your virtual wall to find just the right spot. And shoe sellers are letting you try on a virtual shoe so you can get the perfect look and fit.

As a travel guy, I'm very excited about what AR can do in travel. Think of walking through an ancient city like Rome and having bubbles of information pop around you showing you what the city was like 2,000 years ago.

Picture what it would be like to "seemagine" the proverbial pile of rocks (that every civilization has left behind) and having it come alive so you're experiencing it as it was back then.

I like this idea so much that I've told my game designer son that if he ever gets tired of designing first-person shooter games, I'd fund a company to augment historical monuments using my travel expertise and his gaming props. I hope he takes me up on that offer.

Of course, VR/AR and travel may be a blessing and a curse. It could excite you to take a long-delayed trip or vacation, or it could be so enjoyable you decide to stay home and immerse yourself for a few hours without leaving your chair!

VR/AR are expected to be a $111-billion-dollar industry by 2020, so put on those virtual rose-colored glasses and start dreaming of how your business could be improved through AR.

- Could you reduce your costs and increase the quality of your manufacturing operation by helping workers accurately perform tasks they rarely take on?

- Could you explain your product in ways that are more convincing to your customer by showing them what it will look like in their home or office?

- Could you create an entirely new product that disrupts your industry – such as a virtual tour guide for cities around the world?

As VR and AR are built into our phones and glasses, customers and employees will expect you to use it in your business. And with more and more companies complaining that it is hard to hire skilled workers, perhaps these tools can help create the skills, "on the job."

Perhaps training doesn't sound disruptive but think if your employees could perform maintenance twice as fast as competitors. You'd be able to produce products more quickly and thus have lower costs.

And a suggestion. If you do something like that, refrain from trumpeting your idea at the next industry conference. Perhaps keeping it quiet is a better idea.

At American Airlines one of our savvy fleet schedulers had the idea that we should try flying small 727 jets from Dallas to New York every hour, instead of a Jumbo Jet every 4-5 hours. It reduced travel time for connecting passengers and it turned out we carried more total passengers on the route and made more money. Soon we put the idea in place on many routes.

One day our Chairman burst into our weekly staff meeting clutching a copy of a newspaper in his hand and shouted, "Who was the idiot who described our 'AAirbridge' strategy to the New York Times? What is the advantage of explaining our secret sauce to the industry? Now they will copy it!!!"

Sometimes rather than basking in the kudos of others on your disruptive idea, it is better to simply to quietly reap the profits.

BLOCKCHAIN

"The biggest opportunity set we can
think of over the next decade."

—Bob Greifeld, CEO, Nasdaq

If you have heard of blockchain, you probably think of bitcoin. They are related but actually quite different.

Bitcoin is a "cryptocurrency," a currency not issued or backed by a government where security is provided by a trusted third party (like a central bank) but by an algorithm. That formula is blockchain and its immutable design is what makes it a perfect underlayment for a currency.

Bitcoin is a private currency that right now is thinly traded, and highly speculative. There are dozens of "brands" of bitcoins and fortunes are being quickly made and lost by currency speculators. Because it allows for totally anonymous ownership it has been widely used in "Ransomeware" scams and criminals have collected untold millions in untraceable gains.

Thus, when my stepson told me he was leaving his software startup to join a bitcoin company, I was not thrilled by the risk he was taking. But then explained that his new venture was not a bitcoin currency company but rather a company that reported on the value and future of all bitcoin-related currencies, somewhat like Morningstar does for stocks. "Aha," I said, "reporting on a bubble is much safer than being in the bubble machine."

So now that we've discussed the currency, let's talk about something I believe is much more disruptive: blockchain itself.

Since the technicalities are somewhat daunting, perhaps examples of what it can do might be the best introduction.

A recent Walmart test using blockchain reduced the time required to trace a shipment of mangoes from seven days to two seconds, both saving time and verifying origin.[16]

A New York Times article described Maersk's trial of blockchain to simplify cross-border documentation, as a single freight container shipment can require over 200 different communications. Thus finding, as they did, a "substantial reduction" in costs and improving accuracy is a win-win

I knew blockchain was a serious technology when IBM appointed a Vice President of blockchain (is his business card "immutable" as blockchain is supposed to be?).

Think of business as a chain of events between parties and you'll soon conclude that an immutable chain of custody (like evidence on CSI) between parties might be a very good thing.

Smart contracts are being based on blockchain. In these cases the unbreakable chain allows changes of ownership or payment to be triggered automatically based on predetermined conditions.

Sounds good, right? So how does it work?

Let's talk first about "the old way" things worked. For centuries, at least from the invention of double-entry bookkeeping in the 1300s, centralized ledgers have tracked and validated transactions. Banks, trading houses, and governments provided centralized and trusted sources that validated currencies, transactions and tracked the flow of goods.

The key concepts are *centralized* and *trusted third party*.

Blockchain provides another way.

"It is an open, distributed ledger that can record transactions between two parties efficiently and in a verifiable and permanent way," said the *Harvard Business Review* in 2017.

Bettina Warburg in her excellent Ted Talk calls it, "A public registry of who owns what and who transacts what. It stores the history of custodianship, ownership and location for assets."

So blockchain is *distributed* and *software provides the security*, not a trusted third party.

Each transaction is recorded in a block and each block is connected to the next block and protected with a cryptographic key. This has created a theoretically irreversible and unbreakable chain. Adding a block requires software consensus of all users and once added they cannot be modified or deleted. Since transactions are distributed, they don't have a single point of failure and are very difficult to hack.

If I have, in this explanation, only "shed darkness" on blockchain's technology perhaps that is because how blockchain works is very complex.

The good news is that like electricity or the Internet you don't have to know *how* it works to *put* it to work.

What could happen if we could move data or records from hand to hand without the need for them to be centrally verified or without complex audits or paperwork at each step?

Think about how much easier transactions would be with:

Supply Chain Visibility/Management. Such systems are beginning to be based on blockchain. Parts can be traced from the source (very important to airlines). Food can be traced from the grower. Fish can be tracked from the boat to the grocery bin.

Voting. The Nasdaq trialed shareholder voting in Estonia using blockchain to prevent voter fraud.

Health Records. I always laugh when schlepping or faxing records (who even has a fax anymore?) from doctor to doctor as the US seems to create healthcare security by creating a digital Tower of Babble with systems not designed to communicate but to confuse. Estonia has solved this problem by implementing blockchain-based medical records.

Who will be disrupted by startups implementing blockchain-based solutions?

- Title insurance companies – as the chain can obviate the need for such insurance (or create a new type).

- Lawyers – blockchain-based wills won't be able to be disputed. Escrow could be a thing of the past.

- Illegal fishing – could disappear as volume buyers like Red Lobster insist on "bait to plate" tracking of fish.

- Auditors – may find their demand diminished as transactions become self-auditing.

- Airline maintenance – how many times have you waited once your airplane was fixed for the "paperwork" to be signed off by everyone involved? Blockchain could make that happen in a few seconds. The first airline that does that will get my business.

And completely new products will be created such as:

- Music, photography, and video will embed tracking to ensure artists get paid no matter who plays or shows their product.

- 3D printing CAD files will be locked so only authorized printers can print the part you invented.

- IOT devices will communicate with other IOT "thingies" using blockchain to verify who and what they are talking to creating the "secret handshake" of IOT and locking out hackers.

If your business thrives by reducing friction (you are a customs broker, a title insurance company, an escrow agent), think of how you will survive in a world with instantly provable transactions and no friction.

Or ponder for a minute the relationship between your company, your suppliers, and your customers and how adding blockchain to your business processes might lower cost and increase security … or completely disrupt your business!

A final note on overhyped technologies. Of all the technologies in this book I suspect that blockchain is the most overhyped.

That is not because the technology doesn't work or isn't revolutionary. It is because to make a chained product work, everyone has to agree to use it!

So private blockchains used in corporations or between corporate partners are working well as it is in everyone's interest to join the party.

General-use blockchains (let's say changing land titles) are going to be harder as there are many disparate parties involved. For these types of changes to occur, it's probably going to take government involvement, and certainly in the US that seems unlikely to occur in the near term.

That doesn't mean it is impossible. Estonia is now a "digital country" and has digital voting, digital IDs, health records, digital courts, and more. Hopefully, the example of a digital country will spread as it certainly saves money (Estonia estimates 2% of GDP), increases speed, and greatly improves service to the citizens.

Until then, your company may find it a very innovative, or very disruptive technology – the choice of which is yours!

Business author Seth Godin says, "Earn trust, earn trust, earn trust. Then you can worry about the rest."

Would you say your suppliers and customers trust you? Are you a "digital company" or "digital country?"

If so, kudos. If not, is there a way you could be using blockchain to increase security and trust so they do?

ROBOTICS

"Number 5 is alive!"

—Robot Johnny 5,
from the movie *Short Circuit*

I suspect we can all remember when we first saw a robot.

Mine was "Robby the Robot," a fictional character in the movie *Forbidden Planet* in 1956. I thought he was awesome and felt lucky to receive a Robby model for Christmas that year. He had spinning antenna "ears," claws that operated like hands, and wheels in his boots so he could scoot across the kitchen floor.

In 1956 – partially because of the Jetsons TV show and the futuristic exhibits at the World's Fair – it didn't seem like much of a stretch to imagine that fifty years later, robots would be all over the place.

Today, many of us have never encountered a robot except for perhaps a toy or a Roomba vacuum. Yet they do live among us. There are estimated to be more than 2 million industrial robots at work right now.[17]

Movies and TV make us picture robots as humanoid forms, and indeed Webster's first definition of a robot is "a machine that resembles a living creature in being capable of moving independently and performing complex actions."

However, a secondary definition is "a device that automatically performs complicated, often repetitive tasks (as in an industrial assembly line)." And this is where most of the business focus is today.

Robots today don't have to have all their smarts onboard as they can use mobile communications to reach out to the cloud. They don't have to be preprogrammed for every task as machine learning makes them smart enough to be shown a task and then perform it. They are beginning to match us from a sensory perspective as they can at least somewhat see, touch, taste, smell, and hear.

Robots in industry have been around since the 1960s performing tasks such as welding, painting, and "machine tending" (putting materials in and out of machines).

Together the automotive and electronics industries make up over sixty percent of robot installations in 2018. And these industries are making serious progress at automation. At Nissan's factory in Sunderland, England, 95% of the plant is automated.

When I bought my Tesla, I got an opportunity to tour their factory. I've toured car factories before but was amazed by the number of robots involved here. It was also fascinating to see all the things that were missing – no large gasoline engine to install, just small electric motors, no transmission, no radiator!

I was shown how Tesla had reprogrammed its robots to perform several tasks rather than the common single-task robot. Using AI, industrial robots can now be "shown" a task two or three times and go on to perform it over and over, rather than requiring complex programming.

However, when Tesla attempted to "over-robotize" its Model 3 production, they quickly backtracked to more humans. That was the genesis of Elon Musk's quote, "Humans are underrated." Humans still have some operational advantages. Yet, watch out. Robots aren't perfect yet, but they are gaining.

Even though these robots are not like *Star Trek*'s "Data" android, they still have had a significant impact.

Foxconn, which makes electronics for Samsung and Apple, told the South China Post that robots have replaced 60,000 of its workers.

Robot penetration is much higher in manufacturing in China and Korea than in the US. When I was in China recently, I saw a headline proclaiming, "China will lead in lights-out factories!" Given the amount of Chinese labor that would be replaced by such a move I was shocked, but they have determined to create the future despite the cost.

You would think that a country with high labor costs or a labor shortage would be looking to reduce workers and add robots. For China, with a billion mouths to feed, to be the lights-out, robot disruptor is quite a statement about how far they are willing to go to keep a manufacturing lead.

Some are claiming (and advertising) that their medical robots are far superior to human doctors.

These robots are actually "human assisted" and are an extension of the mechanical hands that have been with us since the 1960s. They offer the doctor superior visualization, enhanced dexterity, and greater precision. But the jury is out on their effectiveness. Many studies have shown little or no improvement in patient outcomes. It seems that patients who have robotic surgery don't, at this time, have faster healing or fewer complications than those with human surgeons.

However, the future should bring patients the choice of a doctor from any location without having to travel there ("the Internet of Skills). Robots performing "telesurgery" have already performed operations with a doctor in New York and the patient in Strasbourg. With millions of people having no access to medical care, perhaps this is the best utilization of these types of robots?

Robots have had more success in other parts of the hospital. Robots are entering rooms vacated by patients and eliminating germs with high-intensity UV rays.

The "germinator," as it's been dubbed, can reduce healthcare-associated infections by 50–100%. Other hospitals are experimenting with robot drug-dispensing devices. At USCF, the $24 million dollar "pill picker" robot has dispensed over 350,000 prescriptions without error while at the same time double-checking drug interactions to ensure patients are helped and not harmed.

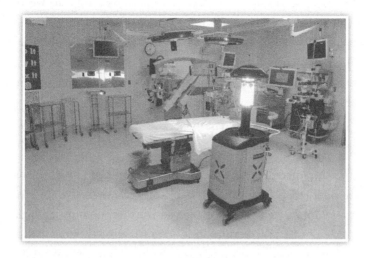

Robots are making significant progress (and sometimes unfortunately replacing humans) in many other sectors.

Warehousing and distribution are becoming intensely robotic with Amazon leading the way. Amazingly, Amazon has just about as many robots (100,000) as employees (125,000).

After buying robot company Kiva, Amazon created a separate division, Amazon Robotics, to create and tailor robotics for distribution. Robots are palletizing, sorting, and moving millions of packages daily. To date, Amazon says robots are not displacing workers, but only because Amazon is growing so fast.

Very similar robots are now sorting suitcases at Heathrow airport in London, perhaps allowing you to go to Milan and your bag to go to Rome, even faster!

There are many robotic trials in farming. Experiments are being deployed in planting, spraying, weeding, and harvesting. The wide diversity of plant life is proving challenging for some of these tasks. It is relatively easy to detect and pick a ripe orange; turns out picking a hot pepper is quite a bit harder. And yet as I write these words, I saw an article stating an experimental robot was able to pick raspberries. Wow! I have trouble getting them out of the box to eat without bruising them.

Machine learning is critical to the success of agricultural robots.

Blueriver Technology is deploying AI-based robotic weed spraying in cotton fields. Using machine learning, the system quickly learned to differentiate weeds from cotton. Now, the system is learning each type of weed, and what herbicide to use to kill each type. This reduces herbicide use by 90% through eliminating broadcast spraying. It also can reduce manpower by almost the same percentage.

Did you know 2% of US cows are milked in an entirely robotic process?

The cows decide when they want to be milked (which turns out to be more often than before). Yes, cows can feel when their udder is full and they voluntarily enter a booth, get scanned for identity, and lasers and pumps do the rest. The result? Production is up 8%. And this proves a boon to dairy farmers as it is increasingly difficult to find workers for this difficult and nonstop job.

I got a chance to see this myself in Iceland. Contented cows ambled in from the pasture, got hooked up, milked and then went back to chewing their cud. There wasn't a farmer in sight!

Sometimes robots aren't physical at all. Some are just code. Enter the "robot reporter." At Bloomberg News, roughly a third of its content is produced by automated means. Financial news is way ahead of other news in using robots. In fact, most breaking news on company financial reports are written by robots.

Having served on seventeen boards of directors, I've always dreaded the task of crafting the earnings reports. There is usually a big debate about what we will emphasize or deemphasize this quarter's press release to put the company in the best light. It is now a losing game. No matter if you talk about new inventions, more customers, greater revenue, the robot author always cuts to the chase and the headline will read, "Loss Widens!"

Of course, robotic auditors may make the boards job easier. Using AI and big data instead of auditors sampling transactions, robot auditors will review *every* transaction to catch errors and fraud, and reduce the board's anxiety.

Robots are also being deployed to perform "discovery" in legal cases, to lay bricks on homesites, to scan documents at insurance firms, and deliver room service in hotels.

Customer-facing robots are coming forward as well. Carnival Cruise lines has a robot bartender; Lowe's, a robot who will find you a product in the store; and in Japan, robots lead exercise routines for seniors.

At my AI company, Wayblazer, we helped Hilton and IBM craft "Connie," a concierge robot. She could listen, talk, and dispense information on the hotel and surrounding things to do. We learned early on that she needed a screen to show guests restaurants and a printer to give them a map. We also learned that hotel lobbies are noisy and at times the robot was a little hard of understanding, particularly with those who did not use English as their primary language.

Although Connie never made it out of proof of concept, I suspect these problems will be solved quickly. For example, an Alexa-like device from MSC Cruises released in 2018 speaks seven languages – Connie (2014) only spoke one.

In retrospect, Connie was probably too early, but Hilton, IBM, and Wayblazer gained learnings for the next project (and got a lot of PR at the same time).

In the view of many people, robots are coming just in time. Headlines every year trumpet that farmers can't find workers to pick fields, and ski resorts where I live in Lake Tahoe can't find seasonal workers. Yet at the same time there is no question that robots will displace numerous workers much as automation has been doing in the coal industry for decades.

So, "lights-out" factories are coming, cows are getting milked on their own, and I suppose robot bartenders are going to have to learn the one about the rabbi, the priest, and the duck who walked into a bar!

It doesn't matter if your business is in manufacturing, agriculture, hospitality, or accounting, you will be working with robots soon.

It is time to put them into your lexicon and technology mix.

Recently I was at a meeting of hoteliers in Hawaii. They were bemoaning the fact that Hawaiian housing is so expensive it is very difficult, if not impossible, for workers to live close enough to their hotels to work there.

Also, many young people simply aren't interested in being housekeepers, bellboys, or restroom attendants. When they mentioned that the *average* age of a housekeeper in their hotels was 61, I said, "Have you thought about robots?" The executives looked at me, dumbfounded. When I pointed out that robots were delivering sheets, towels, and toiletries in hospitals, they had no idea.

My point is that it is time for you to do some robot benchmarking. Take a look at your processes and then go to a robot convention or check Crunchbase or CB Insights for lists of robot startups.

See how robots are building cars, dispensing pills, automating processes (Robotic Process Automation), and disinfecting rooms.

If you're NOT using robots in your organization, it's time to get creative about how they could update your processes and expedite your procedures.

Remember those hotel executives? Robots provided an answer to a problem they thought they didn't have an answer to.

Could robots provide an answer to problems your industry is facing? Here is a short list of business robots. If yours isn't in this list, check online – it probably is by now!

Military	Mining	Security
Hospice Care	Physical Therapy	Agriculture
Home Cleaning	Lawn Care	Bartending
Teaching Assistants	Doctors	Novelists
Pizza Making	Jockey	Robot Design

DATA SCIENCE –
ADVANCED ALGORITHMS –
PREDICTIVE ANALYTICS

*"To some degree every company
will have to become a math house."*

—Ram Charan, Consultant

When *Fortune* magazine titles an article "The Algorithmic CEO," you know that math has come to the forefront of business management.

We have discussed before how big data and AI work together. Now it's time to discuss another related "hot topic" – data science and algorithms.

For a brief time at American Airlines, I was President of AA Decision Technologies, a division that employed over one hundred PhDs in Operations Research. These scientists used advanced mathematical theory to create models that improved airline operations.

Their "tour de force" was a set of programs called Yield Management. These programs optimized how many passengers flew at each price point the airline offered. Obviously, we'd have loved to fill the aircraft with all high-paying passengers, but as that would never happen, we needed help.

Algorithms helped maximize both load (attempting to totally fill the plane) and yield (having the most high-paying passengers possible). It helped route managers to "wait for the guys with ties" – the high payers – but fill the plane with backpackers if they must.

This program was a great success and highly envied by other airlines. Eventually we sold the product. This was a very early example of deploying advanced algorithms to improve corporate results.

Today algorithms are changing all types of businesses.

The most powerful one we use daily is Google Page Rank. You may have forgotten that Yahoo's index of the web was built by hand. Brin and Page at Google built the algorithms that did it automatically. Those "math-men" created a $100-billion-dollar company based on an algorithm.

Here is an unlikely one – thermostats. They had remained unchanged until the energy crises in the 70s pushed the creation of new thermostats that allowed one to program the unit to reduce heating and cooling when you were away. They were difficult if not impossible to program with a range of buttons and features guaranteed to baffle even the technically adept.

Tony Fadell, a former senior VP at Apple, was building a vacation home here in Lake Tahoe and became frustrated by the design idiocy of available thermostats. Using lessons from Apple and advanced analytics, he designed a beautiful and highly functional thermostat that learns from your behavior when to turn the heat up and down. It is so efficient that power companies are giving them away to help reduce power consumption.

Nest is simple, elegant, and powered by math.

Algorithms power Facebook news (for better or worse). Almost 75% of US stocks are traded via automated algorithms. Virtual currencies such as bitcoin and Ethereum are based on blockchain, which is awash in algorithms.

Businesses that deploy data science are seeing dramatic results:

- UPS is saving 85 million driver miles and $2.5 billion in costs by improving driver routing.

- Walmart saved $86 million by designing an algorithm to help staff keep food fresh.

- Red Roof Inns is studying weather patterns to predict cancelled flights and stranded passengers. When the algorithm predicts the right conditions, they push ads such as "Stranded at O'Hare? Check out Red Roof."

Where do data scientists fit in here and who are they? They are "part mathematician, part computer scientist and part trendspotter."[18]

I'd call them the chefs of big data. Think of the data as the ingredients, the algorithms as the kitchen tools, and the data scientist as the chef. They work with the data to produce new outcomes, discover new markets, and improve the bottom line. And importantly these are business functions, not IT functions.

The function of a data scientist is key as they *explain* the data to business managers. My liberal arts college recently started a course in data analytics when they realized how crucial it is becoming to business to have big data interpreters.

Disruptive algorithms require big, clean data so this is another area where established businesses have an edge on startups. Corporations have the data and startups don't.

Many companies are deploying predictive analytics to predict both customer behavior and machine behavior. Predictive maintenance, for example, helps companies determine when their machine is going to fail and get in front of the problem. *IOT Anayltics,* recent research report states that predictive maintenance saved $17 Billion

So how might this all come together for your business and how might you be disrupted by it?

Let's say you have been selling to industry forever. Your product is a sensor that lights a light when a machine fails. Suddenly along comes someone (like Google or Microsoft) who knits together all the data from all the machines in the plant and begins to predict failure. They offer the company "predictive analytics" to tell when that machine your sensor is monitoring is going to fail, rather than just alerting you when it does.

Which product is worth more? *The data-enhanced one, of course.*

Suddenly you are the tail and they are the dog!

Similarly if your company can deploy advanced algorithms to increase yield, reduce cost, save energy, or increase safety, you can disrupt your competition.

Startups don't have as much data as you might, but they can still find data that could disrupt your business.

- TopDogDinners is using data to blend customized dog food for your dog, and we know how particular owners (not dogs) are about dogfood.

- Breath Research makes the 100-year-old stethoscope smart. They call it Shazam for breathing. They are using algorithms to listen to your breath and determine your disease from your breathing pattern.

- Uplift gathers terabytes of consumer finance data to make consumer credit decisions in seconds right when the customer's mouse is hovered over that buy button. Suddenly that $2,000.00 vacation is only $100.00 a month and problem solved.

So, don't think that just having big data is enough. The insights that you gain from it and how you create products from those insights is key.

Working with big data requires patience, skill, and imagination, but using algorithms to find the wisdom in that sea of ones and zeros can create real disruption and big payoffs.

COUNTRIES THAT SKIP – CONSTRAINED RESOURCES

"Life doesn't come with a remote.
You've got to get up and change it yourself."

—A Pinterest Post

After college I had the great good fortune to spend a year travelling around the world. It was so amazing to see how other countries approached things differently than we do in the US.

Having now been in 110 countries, I continue to keep my eyes peeled for differential innovation.

Visiting Africa for the seventh or eighth time recently, I was surprised to see solar panels on the huts in a rural town. A small solar panel is all you need to charge your phone, light LED lights, and even do a small amount of cooking.

Companies like M-KOPA provide solar at costs that save the average (and very poor) user $4 to $5 (KES) weekly on kerosene and phone charging.

It is a funny kind of back to the future. Edison pushed DC power strongly at the beginning of the electric age. Unfortunately, DC cannot be transferred over long distances. Nikola Tesla invented AC power and that allowed for long transmission lines and the developed world strung these lines (at great expense) everywhere. Solar power (which is DC) on every home eliminates the need for transmission lines and infrastructure and most importantly capital.

Similarly Africa has generally skipped over the need for stringing wires to provide phone service, and 93% of Africans have access to cell coverage (vs. 63% with piped water). This has allowed mobile banking company M-Pesa to capture 96% of households in Kenya.[19] Their system doesn't require a smartphone and now poor Kenyans not only have a way to pay but most have a savings account, something that was restricted to high-income residents until recently.

Internet access in India is being provided in some rural communities by the local bus as it drives through town. A few minutes of access a day is all most users require. Google, which is already providing Internet access at railroad stations, is looking to expand access via balloons, and SpaceX and others are racing to deploy thousands of low-altitude satellites to provide worldwide high-speed Internet.

My point is that the developed world spent trillions and took decades to develop the amazing infrastructure we depend on today. The developing world is simply *skipping* it. This could mean that over time things would move faster in the developing world than in the developed world.

It undoubtedly means they approach problems differently. M-Pesa lets anyone bank on a "dumb phone" – something no one in the US does. WeChat's one billion users in China use one app for payments, as a government ID, to buy everything from groceries to cars to booking their doctor's appointment.

As you scan your competitors and new technologies for disruptive forces, be sure that your radar screen includes the developing world; your next disruptor may come from "countries that skip."

Contrary to what you might think, the developing world's lack of resources is not a barrier to innovation.

Over the last few years I've been working for the US Department of State, helping startups around the world. I've met innovators starting companies in Mexico, Malaysia, Iceland and even Outer Mongolia. All of them are innovating on a shoestring.

The phrase "I just don't have the resources" is a perennial lament of the innovator. But sometimes resource constraints are just the ticket to produce great results.

Consider this ...

The recent US mission to Mars cost $730 million dollars and was successful.

The Indian mission to Mars cost a mere $73 million and was also successful.

Why was the Indian mission so cheap? *That's all the money they had!*

Their Mars mission cost less than to produce than the movie *Martian* (which cost $100 million)!

Lack of infrastructure and limited funds don't seem to stop committed disruptors; don't let them stop you.

Astronaut Buzz Aldrin said, "Mars is there, waiting to be reached."

To paraphrase Buzz, disruption is there, waiting to leveraged.

CUSTOMERS

"The only thing moving faster than
technology is customer expectations."

—Jeffery Kabuki, CEO, Fiserv

Customers are also a disruptive force. Kabuki's quote is spot on.

Customers today are Internet-empowered, time savvy, and information rich.

They want what they want when they want it. And increasingly that is 24 × 7 × 365.

Business schools used to teach that companies should choose between low touch, low price, wide selection vs. high touch, high price, and limited selection. Now it seems companies not only can, but must be low price, wide selection, and high touch.

Today's customers expect you to use technology to:

- Show them what's popular
- Help them focus in
- Get to know them
- Spark their imagination
- Listen and learn from them

Consumers have gained enormous power through the vast trove of information on the web. Prices are have become transparent, competitive choice is a click away, and location is meaningless. The brand no longer creates product consideration; that now comes from the reviews of others.

Speed and convenience seem to trump all other attributes.

How did Dollar Shave Club garner 51% of the online shaving market? By having a razor show up at your house automatically a few times a month – speed and convenience.

Customers are also highly attracted to products that are EASY.

Everyone wants more features.

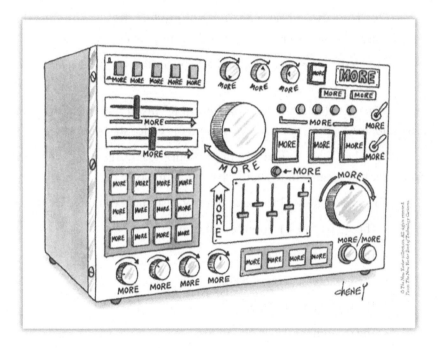

No one wants more complex interfaces.

My Tesla

- Opens the door when I step up to the car
- Closes the door when I step on the brake
- "Starts" the car when I sit in the driver's seat (no start button)
- Turns on the lights when it is dark (there is no button)

- Turns on the wipers when it rains
- Lowers the car at high speed for less drag
- Opens the garage door when I drive up (no button)
- Locks the door and uses its cameras to watch for bad guys when I leave
- Adds new features and fixes problems via Wi-Fi with no intervention

That's more features and more simplicity. And when your product is this feature rich and simple you don't need to advertise (You've never seen a Tesla ad!).

Cars have always been a depreciating product. Tesla is a product that "appreciates" in customer value as it adds features over time.

My Nest thermostat adjusts the temperature when I leave; I don't program it.

When I tell Alexa to turn on "morning" my drapes open, the lights come up, the security system goes off, and my coffee starts brewing.

Yet when I call United Airlines I shout "Agent, Agent, Agent" at the robot because it can't understand what I want to do.

To compete for and win 21st century customers you must have:

- The speed and selection of Amazon
- The simplicity of Nest
- The personalization of Netflix
- The immediacy of Uber
- The customer service of Zappos
- The user interface of Tesla

Many companies are still trying to figure out how to implement CRM, how to move from distributors to Direct to Consumer (D2C), and how to make their products smart.

I'd encourage all of them to step on the gas.

Because in the 21st century you will have to determine how to:

- Express your brand via AI

- Show your product via VR

- Personalize your product via big data

- Make your robot as friendly as the Pillsbury Dough Boy

And much, much more.

Sam Walton said it best, "There is only one boss. The customer. And he can fire everybody in the company from the chairman on down, simply by spending his money somewhere else."

On a scale of 1–10, how would you rate your customer interaction? More importantly, how would *your customers* rate you?

If you benchmark against the best, those who are deploying tech to improve the customer experience, do you fall short? If so, the customer may vote you out of office with a mouse click.

SECTION II –
BUSINESS MODELS

In the preceding chapters we've discussed what I believe are *the most* disruptive technologies impacting business. There are other game changers including:

- Nanotechnology
- Biotechnology and gene splicing
- Quantum computing
- Self-landing rockets

However, it's time to move on to show how these disruptive technologies are changing customer relationships and creating new business models. Then, we'll move on to specific actions you can take to avoid being disrupted.

Let's get to it.

OWN THE EDGE – WIN THE GAME

"We live on the edge of the miraculous."

—Henry Miller, Playwright

At a conference long ago, I heard someone say, "Technique follows technology."

It's an insightful statement. It takes time for us to really find the best use of each new technology.

Alexander Graham Bell thought the telephone would be a tool for the deaf. Edison thought his record player would succeed as a dictation machine. In both cases the market found a different application.

Businesses today are using finding technologies that are upending traditional business models and customer relationships.

Tom Godwin's famous quote from TechCrunch says it best:

- "Uber (the world's largest taxi company) owns no vehicles.
- Facebook (the world's largest publisher) develops no content
- Alibaba (the world's largest retailer) has no inventory.
- Airbnb (the world's largest hotel chain) owns no real estate."

What do they own?

They own the edge.

The "edge" in business used to be location, having your shop at First and Main. Businesses fought to get the best location. McDonalds and Starbucks still use enormous computing power to find the best location for their stores.

But the Edge has moved.

Today the edge is the edge of the glass.

That's because the edge of the glass is where the customer lives, whether she's shopping the in the store or relaxing at home. The edge is the screen we are all swiping and staring at for hours per day.

The average US adult spends four hours a day looking at their smartphone screen._

APPS are of course a huge part of the new EDGE.

Taco Bell recently announced that they get a 20% higher average order value from the APP then in the store. Why? Because with the APP you can see all the items they sell not just the twenty most popular on the backboard. In addition, buying with the APP is not rushed; there is no pressure from the guy behind you who is in a hurry!

Domino's has revitalized itself over the last ten years; its stock price is up $20 to over $200!

A great deal of that had to do with simply making better pizza, but their digital operation helped mightily as well.

Domino's now employs more people in IT than any other corporate department. Their digital sales are over 60% of their orders.

One of the key reasons (and I'll come back to this theme again and again) is they used technology to make it EASY.

Their APP is not only tap and buy, but they added an inspection feature so you can see the pizzas progress to your door. From "on the fire" to "in the car" you know exactly when you can eat.

By understanding that customers today want speed and convenience over almost every other attribute, they stole the edge from Pizza Hut.

Speed and convenience are the reason almost one half of US households pay over $100 annually for two-day shipping and other conveniences with Amazon Prime.

Waze, the traffic app, garners traffic data by monitoring the movements of its over 90 million app users. Now they are beginning to monetize their edge position by understanding when you are stuck in traffic and offering alternatives. No, I don't mean alternative routes as they have done that for years; they now will note your position and say, "You are going to be stuck here for a while. Need a doughnut? There's a Dunkin Donuts on the next corner!"

General Motors and IBM Watson announced something similar. By monitoring GPS location and even seat sensors to see how many people are in the car, GM is offering coupons for nearby locations. Or they might notice you are low on gas, suggest an Exxon station, and offer to let you pay from your car's entertainment display using a MasterCard. In this case, the car is the EDGE.

Amazon began experimenting with advanced EDGE products when it launched the Dash button. It's a tiny Wi-Fi enabled and Amazon connected button that you could stick on your washing machine, for example, and simply push it when you needed more Tide. There were dozens of these buttons for a large variety of items like dog food, paper towels, and toilet paper. While they weren't a smash hit, they provided lots of learning. Amazon has since moved past EDGE buttons to release Dash Replenishment Services. By offering an application interface to household appliance manufacturers, they can build their edge device into someone else's machine!

So my Britta now orders its own filters, my Brother printer orders its own ink and my washer will soon order its own Tide! What a lock-in. Think you will bother to reprogram your Britta to order from Target? No, and in any case, Target doesn't even do this.

Owning the EDGE is a super powerful strategy that companies are using to get closer and closer to the customer.

UPS is worried that 3D printers in the home will replace the need for the UPS truck to stop by. So they are putting 3D printers in their stores. At least you will stop by!

Amazon has taken that one step further by filing a patent for 3D printers in a delivery truck. They will print the thingy you ordered while the truck is driving to your house! Talk about speed and convenience.

Kayak has over 60 million APP users. We stole the edge from the travel providers by offering a mobile app that is faster and more powerful than they provide. This allows Kayak to charge travel suppliers for delivering customers to them. That's the power of owning the edge.

Losing the edge can mean losing your customers and that is painful.

A couple of years ago I spoke to a group of the largest Electrical Utilities in the world. The other speakers were representatives of Tesla, Solar City, and Nest.

The utilities loved Nest (as it saved power), loved Tesla (as it consumes power), and hated Solar City (because it was power!).

In my talk, I explained that I was confused by their hesitation in selling solar power systems to consumers. Certainly I understood that their traditional model required huge central plants, complex transmission lines, and lot of labor to keep it all going.

What I could not understand was their failure to grasp that they were losing the edge by not selling solar.

I am a Solar City customer. The solar panels I own create so much energy that at the end of the year SDGE pays me and I don't pay them. Even though I remain connected to the SDG&E grid for power when the sun goes down, I no longer think of myself as an SDG&E customer. I manage my power use thru an app, and at the end of the year SDG&E pays me for the power I sell them. *Update:* I just installed a Tesla battery and I no longer need SDG&E at night. I charge the battery during the day and discharge it when its dark.

Why aren't these companies selling solar panels? Customers certainly want them. It could be a profitable business and they could smartly manage the transition to a renewable world (coming whether they want to believe it or not).

It seemed from our discussion that they were in "the central power generation business," not the power business.

At countless business conferences I've attended, someone always berates the railroad companies for not understanding they were in the business of transporting people (rather than being a railroad) and thus adding air travel to their portfolio.

It's a great example for a speech, yet there are few examples of those who pull it off.

One savvy power company just might, Green Mountain power in Vermont. Their strategic plan states that they will:

- Change from the old energy system of centralized, fossil-fuel-based generation transmitted through traditional poles and wires to customers far away, toward lower carbon, renewable, distributed generation with new, complex local and regional grid management opportunities.

- Change from one-way electricity flowing from a central plant to a customer toward two-way energy information, storage, and delivery between customers and us to benefit all.

Green Mountain is convincing customers who use natural gas to switch to solar and eliminating expensive rural transmission lines.

They are even renting Tesla batteries to customers for a paltry $15 per month (Tesla charges $10,000 for them). Why? Well it produces backup power for the customer (no generator required) but Green Mountain uses them as part of the deal to provide peak power during hot summer days. The customer's batteries at the edge are knitted together to create a giant, additional power plant!

There are a myriad of other examples from Penny, Mint, and Yodlee handling millennial banking needs using data from big banks, to Uber's software stealing the customers from uncounted taxis.

The point is: think about how you can use these new technologies to ensure you don't lose your edge, or how you can capture the edge from someone else.

- Can you lock in orders for your consumables by building in automatic ordering? Remember Kaeser selling Air as a Service?

- Can you make it so easy to order and monitor shipping, as Domino's did, that 60% of your orders are digital?

- Can you focus on customer needs rather than "what we've always sold" and capture more of the edge as Green Mountain Power is doing?

- Can you make your edge product so fast and easy you capture 60 MILLION customers who'd rather shop with you rather than an airline as Kayak did?

- Can you combine your sensors with very smart software based on big data so Google won't steal your industrial edge – like Honeywell?

If you don't, then two guys and a dog from Silicon Valley are going to figure out how to steal your edge and eat your lunch.

OPA – OTHER PEOPLE'S ASSETS

"A startup is not a smaller version of a large company.
They not only create new products,
they create new business models."

—Steve Blank, Cofounder, E.piphany

Somewhere out there in Silicon Valley is a group of entrepreneurs getting ready to come after your business.

Their slogan? "Your margin is our opportunity."

VCs deployed a staggering $100 billion in 2018 in over 8,000 startups.

While it is still true that eight out of ten fail, the others are gunning for you.

They not only move fast, they move in different ways and along the way create new business models.

After I left Travelocity, I went to work for a Venture Capital firm and looked at many potential travel investments. We looked at a startup that was doing price comparison and found it interesting. It was a browser plugin (we didn't like that) that could detect when you were on one travel site and open another window that showed you results from others. It was slow, clunky, required a download, but the germ of a great business was there.

One night we had the classic "dinner and a napkin" meeting. Former executives of Orbitz, Expedia, Travelocity and the VC partner gathered together to discuss the concept and sketch it out on a napkin.

The business problem was that 96% of the customers of each our sites visited but in the end didn't buy. They were simply using us to compare price and then went somewhere else to buy (usually direct to the airline or hotel). "What if," we said, "we build a site that searches everything but when you click … you buy direct?"

We created a very slim and extremely fast layer between the customer and the supplier that provided what the customer was looking for … choice of where to buy.

That little idea garnered 60 million downloads and stole the edge from the suppliers. It would be worth $1.8 billion.

The key was that it made the shopping process *much* simpler for the buyer.

It also had a very simple business model.

Here is the Travelocity business model:

Travelocity

Find Clients	Search for Products	Book Ticket
Issue Ticket	Issue Itinerary	Bill & Collect
Post Sale Service	Pay Airline	Deal with Retuns

Here is Kayak's:

Simple and quite disruptive.

Another example of creating a simple model is the change that Jeff Bezos made at Amazon to begin selling used books. I am sure to the team it initially seemed like a crazy idea. Who sells used and new of the same thing in the same store? I guess only car dealers. But new cars are quite different from used ones. Used books, not so much.

But look at the difference in business model. Here is Amazon's traditional model

Amazon Traditional

Buy Book	Set Price	Finance Inventory
Store Book	Find Clients	Market Book
Ship Book	Sell Book	Bill Collect

and here is the used book model

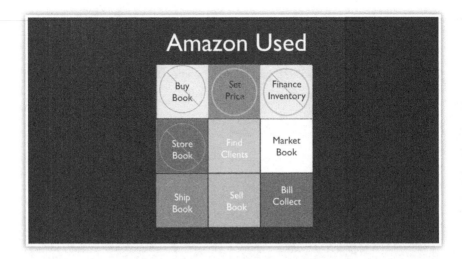

With the new model they don't have to acquire the book, store the book, finance the inventory, price the book, nor ship the book.

Amazon never acquires the asset which means that even though the absolute dollars brought home are small, the margins are excellent.

Over time this idea morphed into Fulfillment by Amazon (FBA) where the seller of any product can list and sell their products on Amazon, and even store their goods in Amazon's warehouse and take advantage of Prime shipping. This is now a $9-billion-dollar part of Amazon's retail business.

Uber follows the same plan. Here is the traditional limo business model

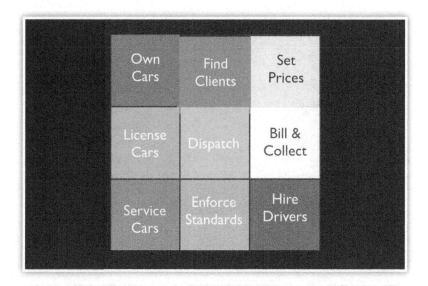

Here is Uber's

They don't own cars, license cars or service cars. They don't enforce brand standards; the customer does that through reviews. They don't have to find and hire drivers; the drivers find them.

They just do four things really well: find clients; set prices; dispatch; bill and collect. Top it off with wonderful easy to use software at the EDGE and become the biggest limo company on the planet. And create a company today worth more than GM or Ford.

Airbnb follows the same game plan.

The traditional hotel:

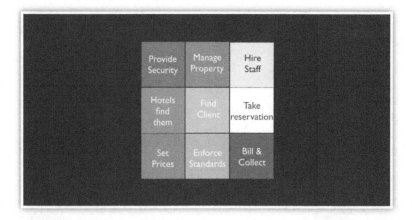

Airbnb

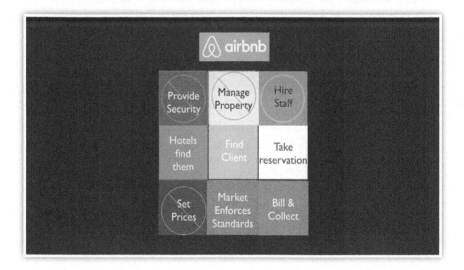

Airbnb doesn't manage the property, hire staff, provide security, or set prices. Hotels find them and the market enforces their standards.

Layer on some great software and you have the largest hotel company on Earth.

When I was asked to speak at the American Limo Association about innovation, I knew what the first question after the speech would be, "How do we beat Uber?"

The answer was simple. "Get some bloody software!" They already had the asset (cars), driver, customers, and brand; they were just way more difficult to deal with than Uber. (Like my friend Ed in the introduction.)

Uber stole the edge and won much of the market. The corporate limo market is still up for grabs but in my opinion the incumbents still don't understand how hopelessly behind they are.

I get it. It is very hard to give up what's worked for so many years. In 2003 I was asked to speak about innovation to a Yellow Pages Association. I thought, "This is a zombie Industry. They are dead but they don't know it." I briefly considered that my entire speech should consist of, "Ladies and Gentlemen, YOU are TOAST." But they were paying me lots of money so I took about an hour to weave it together for them J

In looking at these models you may say (as the Yellow Pages certainly did), "Well this simply isn't fair. I have the factory, the supply chain, the distributors, and the brand!"

Maybe so. But are you EASY?

There is a saying in Silicon Valley, "Step one, install software. There is no step two."

That's easy.

And that is what Kayak and Uber and Airbnb are – drop-dead easy, a click or two and you are done. They have the speed and convenience the customer demands today.

And to top it off, they have hardly any assets.

They are about LESS CAPITAL and MORE SPEED.

Their business model is a shining example of why it's so smart to leverage Other People's Assets (OPA).

However, don't stop there. In our next chapter, you'll discover ways to leverage Other People's Information (OPI).

OPI – OTHER PEOPLE'S INFORMATION

"Where is the wisdom we have lost in knowledge?
Where is the knowledge we have lost in information?"

—T. S. Elliot, Poet

Platforms exist that simply broker information. Google is the best example of exploiting OPI or "Other People's Information."

Think of the range of business information they give you access to (much of it collected by others at great cost).

- News
- Stocks
- Hotels
- Airlines
- Images
- Shopping
- Books

By indexing that information and selling placement they created a massive business.

This is a model I've worked with for a long time.

SABRE, the reservation computer at American Airlines, is one of the earliest examples of monetizing corporate information.

American (and other airlines) placed their reservations systems with travel agents to help agents book flights and sell tickets.

Each system listed their host carrier first. For example, in SABRE when you asked for flights from Chicago to New York, the first screen listed only American flights. Then you saw flights from airlines that paid to be listed next. Finally you saw everyone else. Since American subsidized the system, we felt it was our right to list AA first and obviously we got more reservations this way.

Eventually the Justice Department stepped in and said we could not "bias" our displays in this way. We asserted that it wasn't bias, it was simply "Alphabetical Order" (AA) J, but since United could not make that claim, the government won and we "unbiased" our display.

That ruling could have created a bad ending to our project, but instead it turned out to be a godsend. The ruling said we could not "bias" the display, but it did allow us to charge the other airlines for participation in our platform. Since we had already placed our systems in thousands of travel agencies, we already owned the edge in this market. The other airlines had to participate in SABRE. We charged for every reservation we made for them and overnight SABRE was a $1-billion-dollar company!

In fact, for a time, the SABRE division (using American's and others' data) was worth more than the airline.

James Jones, a retail analyst at RBC, put it best, "The battle is decided if the startup gets the distribution before the incumbent gets the innovation." And that is exactly what happened with SABRE.

Please think about that quote for a minute. Think about how disruptive that statement is. Customers got Uber or Lyft software initially for use in one city but then as they travelled and more locations were added they could use it everywhere.

It was Apple's success with the iPod and iPhone that gave it the power to push music producers to "by the song" pricing.

Kayak too followed this rule. Our idea (as outlined in the previous chapter) was to let customers compare all airline or hotel prices and then buy direct. And since all their shopping was completed when they clicked, we wouldn't take them to the first page of AA or DL, we take them to the "buy" page. Thus, our customer's click (as they had already selected their product) was much more valuable than a Google click, where they were just dumped on the home page.

The airlines loved it. "Much better than that Travelocity commission model," they said. But even so they refused to pay a penny for our service!

So, with VC funding, we built the product anyway and began sending them lots and lots of traffic. The airlines were soon addicted to our very high converting customers.

Then one day we simply turned the system off! Our phones rang off the hook. "Where is our traffic?" one airline boss ranted. We replied, "Same place your money is ... nowhere!"

They paid up. (Did we invent Ransomware? J)

You will recall that Google started without a business model. It was only after they had the traffic that the ad model made sense.

Today there are hundreds of vertical search platforms, for shopping, music, podcasts, video, lawyers, and more.

Starting a vertical search engine is very difficult. It's hard to get competitors to join and to attract customers. Think of a giant ancient mill wheel. Very hard to start, but very efficient when up to speed.

Many companies are thinking of starting vertical search in their industry. I've given advice to companies in farming, retail, even one in the gravel business. Turns out there many different types of gravel and the pricing is quite opaque, thus a great place for search.

You may find, as American did, that the data about your business can be worth more than the business itself.

The point is, as Shirley Chisholm said, "You don't make progress by standing on the sidelines, complaining. You make progress by implementing ideas."

Is your organization on the sidelines when it comes to leveraging data, or are you building a platform that collects and accumulates data you can then leverage with customers or sell to other markets?

And why we're on the subject, also keep your antenna up for how you can leverage Other People's Products (OPP) and Other People's Data (OPD).

A classic example of OPP is the iTunes store. Jobs convinced the music labels to sell by the song rather than the album (who wanted the "B" side anyway?). At peak they were selling about $3 billion in music downloads.

A great example of OPD is Waze. They collect data from their 50 million users to determine traffic delays and best routing. Then they "sell" it back to you. In this case you aren't charged, but you do see ads.

Many of the startups being deployed today are based on the "platform model" where they leverage all the O's – OPA, OPI, OPP, and OPD.

You start with one thing that attracts customers and then use your "platform" and the "O's" to sell them many goods and services.

Or you can sell them something over and over. That's next.

OAO – OVER AND OVER – SUBSCRIPTIONS AND SAAS

"Membership has its privileges."

—American Express

As you'll discover in this chapter, customers will give us their trust and their ongoing loyalty if we build a subscription community they want to be part of.

The subscription business model has been around a long, long time. Magazines and newspapers are the most common examples. You could even say we "subscribe" to water or trash pickup as they have a monthly charge.

In today's business world "XAAS" something as a service usually means that rather than selling you a machine that produces compressed air, I'll sell you air by the volume you consume, rather than a CD Rom and you own the software, I'll rent it to you by the seat and deliver it via the cloud.

SAAS subscription billing of course is very similar to traditional software annual subscriptions in that one is billed monthly or annually … but the comparison breaks down after that.

SAAS means buyers don't need computer infrastructure, long installation times, or consultants to help with implementation. All this makes

SAAS an easier sale and it is simple to try before buying. Customers are always on the latest software version as there is only one version online.

Of course, no installation and monthly billing mean it is easy to cancel as well, which is why SAAS companies have large "customer success" teams to help avoid that trap.

But the most interesting change to me is the real-time learnings that come from having the customer constantly connected to the software. We quickly learned this at Travelocity and Kayak, because they were web sites which provide lots of user feedback. Many traditional "on premise" software companies don't have that learning loop, and they suffer the consequences as a result.

Like our example earlier of Netflix, who "watches" what people are watching, SAAS companies identify which parts of the software people use heavily and which parts are ignored. They also can pinpoint where customers get stuck in a baffling part of their interface – and can fix it accordingly.

I began speaking about the benefits of subscription model years ago in my speech on Building Digital Relationships. I encouraged the groups I spoke with to consider using their online sites to begin a subscription relationship with their customers. From dog food to diapers, we all need things over and over again. Amazon is brilliant at this, yet I'm surprised how many other companies are not taking advantage of this profitable process.

The subscription model not only delivers an annuity revenue stream and customer knowledge, selling directly lets you turn the traditional distribution model on its head.

Tien Tzuo in his wonderful book *Subscribed* digs deep into this change. I'm not totally in agreement with his model, so I'm taking some liberties with it, but here is the essence.

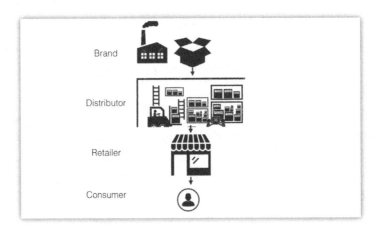

This worked very well. Proctor and Gamble, one of the most savvy brands on earth, has been selling Ivory soap since 1837 and Gillette (now part of P&G) razors since 1900. With the model above, they were able to build strong national brands, reap huge economies of scale and lead their categories.

They pushed massive amounts of products through distributors and retailers. And while they built loyalty, no one in the chain could or did build an ongoing relationship with their customers.

The subscription model looks like this:

In this model the customer (now a subscriber) is at the center. They are surrounded by omni channels where they can learn more about and subscribe to the products that surround the channels.

And obviously, the brand surrounds all.

To me, this model lets the physical brand work more like an online brand. Through the subscription, sellers are constantly connected to the subscriber and can learn their tastes and create new offerings that are in alignment with their preferences.

Dollar Shave Club is a good example of how this works.

The razor business has been in a tech war for a long time (I've had a beard for 50 years, so I know this only from friends J),

One blade went to two, two to four, then to six. They added titanium, flexibility, lubrication, and other flummery and suddenly you have a product that costs $0.40 cents to manufacture but sells for $19.95 (for four cartridges).

Dollar Shave Club introduced a new and better option. They created a subscription model that sold a "humble" twin blade razor and 5 cartridges a month for $3.00 per month, and had upgrades from there. They worked hard to create a "club" atmosphere. They included small gifts in their packages, had lot of shaving tips on their website, and even included a monthly magazine in their shipments.

By getting to know their customers through purchase information, samples, and direct and email offers DSC began expanding its offerings to include shave creams, shampoos, hair creams, lip balm and more.

In a few years DSC captured over $200 million of the shaving market, had 3.5 million members, and only 190 employees. They did this while fighting Gillette's $1.4 billion in sales and 30,000 employees.

That is the power of subscription marketing. It's also an example of what my friend Hemant Taneja describes as *Unscaled* (in his book of the same name).

DSC didn't need P&G's scale to compete. It bought outsourced razors for a few pennies more than P&G's cost, built its brand for peanuts on YouTube and via WOM, didn't pay fees to distributors and retailers, and leveraged its relationship to sell more to each customer while earning a recurring revenue stream. Nice!

DSC was purchased in 2016 for $1 billion in cash. Gillette recently cut the price of their blades by 20%![20]

As Tzuo notes, "Competitors can steal your product features, but they can't steal the insights you gain from your active and loyal subscriber base."[21]

Key point: you have to listen and act on those insights!

Traditional companies are picking up on this idea.

- Husqvarna offers the battery box. A large shipping-container-like box sits in Swedish Home Improvement store parking lots. Inside are a range of heavy power tools like trimmers, saws, and blowers. You rent with an app, pick up from a locker, and return when you are done. All for a monthly subscription.

- SNCF (the French railroad) created online subscriptions for travelers. For a fixed fee you can get unlimited travel.

- Volvo created CARE, a car subscription. You get the car, but also insurance, maintenance (with pickup), tires, even access to a larger or smaller car for short periods.

- *Motor Trend* magazine started producing video content for YouTube and turned that into a subscription model that is now producing half their revenue.

Subscriptions are about "access vs. ownership".[22] It's important to note that subscription companies are growing nine times faster than the S&P 500.

Are you exploring how your organization could set up a subscription system for your services and products?

If so, great.

If not, why not?

ONI – OUTCOMES NOT IRON

> "The biggest impediment to a company's
> future success is its past success."
>
> —Dan Schulman, CEO, PayPal

ONI – Outcomes Not Iron – is the model where traditional business can fight back against the disruptors.

This is where your past success doesn't have to impede your future success – unless you let it.

Let's define what we are talking about.

I first got involved with outcomes in several speaking engagements for Honeywell.

We all know Honeywell for their ubiquitous thermostats, but they also sell a myriad of industrial sensing products, fire protection systems, and much more.

In listening to their customers and watching the advancements in IOT, Honeywell became convinced that their customers wanted much more than a sensor that turned on a red light on a console when something went wrong.

Customers wanted to move from sensing to meaning to outcomes.

For example, let's say there is a sensor on an air conditioning compressor that detects overheating. In the old days that sensor would light a lamp on some console that hopefully was seen by an operating engineer.

The engineer then had to:

- Determine what the red light meant (meaning)

- Take action (shut down the compressor)

- Determine what process would be affected (no AC in section 4)

- Take further action (turn on backup compressor)

- Determine who could service the problem and get them dispatched

In industry 4.0, the compressor sensor should send data to a process system that could take all the steps outlined above and inform the company about both the problem and the solution.

And Honeywell's latest systems do just that.

Now instead of just selling the sensor (iron) they sell an outcome (uninterrupted air conditioning).

With predictive analytics added to this scenario, the outcome gets more interesting.

Analytics and better sensors could allow them to sell compressor uptime, by predicting when a failure might take place and performing condition-based maintenance to prevent it.

GE is doing exactly that and selling jet and locomotive engines by the hour. You want 95% uptime; well that costs X, 99% uptime quite a lot more. But you don't buy the engine; you buy the uptime. As they put it, "Engines talk, we listen."

Imagine if someone came to your company and said, "I will guarantee that I can increase the output of your warehouse 10% and the risk is on me." Or rather than selling you paint someone would paint your cars. Or if you use my fertilizer and analytics exactly as specified (and we have IOT to check) I will guarantee your crop output! (BTW these are all actual examples)

Companies are today selling outcomes like increased productivity, decreased energy usage, increased safety, or decreased maintenance.

Selling outcomes is very different than selling iron. I've worked with many resellers who had to move from selling servers to selling cloud services.

They had to stop selling speeds and feeds to technical buyers and begin selling outcomes to digitally empowered leaders. These sales move from selling purchasing to selling the CXO, so think about the training you will have to give the salesforce if you adopt these models.

Outcomes are a fast-growing choice of companies who are digitally enabling their products.

It's become clear to them that the data and services surrounding their product can create an annuity business that can be extremely profitable (see subscriptions above).

Think what happens if you just keep selling iron. Your product becomes a very replaceable sub part of a much larger system. Google, Microsoft, or someone else can spec the parts of the system because they are the ones determining the outcome.

Statesman David Lloyd George said, "He has sat on the fence so long, the iron has entered his soul."

Don't be content to sit on the fence. It's not enough to own the iron.

You must own the edge, and you also must own assets and the outcome.

SO WHAT'S YOUR NEW MODEL?

"Time may not be on our side, but innovation is."

—Fans van Houten, CEO, Royal Phillips

We've discussed a variety of innovative technologies and business models that, hopefully, have been food for thought.

I'm sure by now you've seen how easy it is to be disrupted.

So, what to do? Can you hide from this tsunami? Can you hold it back?

The day Kodak went bankrupt, Instagram raised a billion dollars.

Photography didn't go away, Kodak did. You can't hide nor wait.

Microsoft's Office was always a cash cow for the company. It dominated its category for years. But when the cloud and SAAS came about, Office got killed by Google Docs. Google took share like crazy.

Yet time *was* on the side of Office. Just a few years later, Office pulled into the lead. It is now one of the biggest cloud apps of all. How did they do that?

They did some very un-Microsoft like things. They converted Office to run on iPhone iOS and Android. They partnered with Box and Dropbox, *even though they sell a competitive product.*_

It was painful, and they are making less revenue per sale. But they're not only still in the game; they're winning the game!

A few years ago, I was asked to speak on innovation to the Hartford Steam Boiler Inspection and Insurance Company. They were founded in 1866 just after the Civil War when a boiler explosion on a Mississippi steamer took 1,800 lives.

"Wow," I thought, "selling the same product after 150 years, I'll bet they're ready for some innovation."

In the pre-speech call that I do before every major presentation, I asked their CEO what they were doing that was new and different.

"Well," he replied, "We just got into cyber insurance and bought an IOT company!"

Suffice it to say, I was impressed. This is a company that isn't going to be disrupted. They understand their core strengths. For 150 years they have been inspecting industrial machines to help prevent failure and provide insurance to pay for those inevitable ones.

IOT devices will need inspection and insurance. Cyber requires inspection, shared best practices, and insurance.

Hartford Steam Boiler Inspection and Insurance didn't have to change their model; after all inspection and insurance are in their name.

They just had to *reimagine* how to apply their skills to an entirely new world of products. And in doing so, they moved way beyond boilers.

They've got both time *and* innovation on their side. Do you?

REIMAGINE (SUMMATION OF PARTS I AND II)

"Everything is impossible until somebody does it."

—Bruce Wayne (Batman)

The previous chapters have outlined what I believe are the most important technological innovations happening today, and given an overview of some of the business models emerging around them.

I hope these examples rocked you back on your mental heels and got you thinking about how you might respond.

We all know that tomorrow won't be like today. We should be preparing for the future instead of bemoaning it, reimagining it instead of seeing it as impossible.

We promise ourselves we'll tackle these looming issues, but then we're barraged with incoming emails and crises. We end up subsumed by the urgency of now.

Take 5 minutes right now to be a visionary on behalf of your organization. Imagine what your company's future *could* be by deploying these disruptive technologies.

Envision specific ways you could create a competitive edge or increased market-share by being the first to employ these new business models.

Continuing your SOPs – standard operating procedures – is a prescription for obsolescence. You must *reimagine* how to adapt your policies, products, and procedures so they're current. For example:

- Reimagined crop dusters not only spray chemicals on crops, they now tell farmers where to deploy more water and more fertilizer.

- Reimagined 3D printers not only make parts, they are printing prosthetic hands for kids who didn't grow hands; they are printing skin right over burns.

- Reimagined light fixtures are beaming out Wi-Fi, sensing intruders, playing music, and answering questions by incorporating Alexa.

At a critical moment in WWII, General George Patton said he had "precisely the right instrument … at precisely the right moment … in exactly the right place."

It is highly probable you do as well *if* you take time right now to start creating what could be instead of continuing what is.

Review these technologies. Use them as a springboard to change the game. Brainstorm with your team how you can update your business model to learn instantly from your customers. Strategize how you can reduce cost and increase utility at the same time to give your company a competitive edge.

Why, at age 70, do I travel the world speaking on innovation and disruption?

Because I believe that disruption and innovation <u>are</u> two side of the same coin.

Because companies need to wake up and move past the pinball machine of indecision.

They need to adapt and adopt the technologies we've discussed.

You only call it a disruption because you didn't do it!

The upcoming chapters will show you how to do it with a variety of proactive prescriptions that will help you change SOP – for good.

WHAT ELSE MUST WE DO TO AVOID DISRUPTION?

"Companies rarely die from moving too fast."

—Reed Hastings, CEO, Netflix

By now you may be thinking, "It isn't a question of *if* my industry will be disrupted, but *when*."

"Good on you. You've been paying attention."

It may help to remember this isn't the first time disruption has changed the game.

- In 1900 the top five companies by market cap were industrial or food companies.

- By 2018 all five were software: in order, Apple, Amazon, Microsoft, Alphabet, and Facebook.

We bemoan (rightly) the loss of manufacturing jobs in the US, but don't forget our great great grandfathers were mostly farmers.

Almost 40% of us lived on farms in 1900. Today 1% do.

Almost 30% of us worked in manufacturing in 1920. Today it is less than 8%.

By the way, it's important to understand that in both sectors, output is at an all-time high today. What's that mean? The people went away, the industry didn't.

Automation changed both industries. The automated assembly line paid more than the farm and people moved to town. Now, more efficient operations and robotics have increased manufacturing output while reducing manpower.

There has been lots of talk over the past few years about the "war on coal" decreasing jobs for miners. But the real story is somewhat different. There were 800,000 miners in the US in 1920, but only 80,000 by 2000 (long before the "coal wars").

What caused the decline in workers? Automation.

And coal output increased during that the entire time period.

It's easy to forget these types of cycles happen over and over.

Coal Miners, Telephone Operators, Blockbuster Video Workers, the list goes on and on.

During my early career, travel agents went from 50% share of airline tickets to close to 80%. After airlines were deregulated, that fell dramatically to about 17% today.

Like death, disruption comes for everyone sooner or later.

If you think your industry is immune, may I offer one penultimate example?

The funeral industry.

A recent report detailed that digitization of funeral purchases in Berlin has cut industry revenue by two thirds! The Berlin funeral industry was a kind of club where everyone had a tacit agreement not to cut prices. But then, funerals went online and the new entrants didn't agree with that idea. They wanted volume and had reduced costs though online marketing so they chopped prices and the funeral dirge played for the old guard.[23]

So, what can we do about the disruptions that are coming for us?

When I was a VP at American Airlines, I was invited to take part in a strategic planning exercise.

A group of ten VPs was selected for the exercise. We assembled off-site in a hotel and were met by a team of external consultants.

We knew we were going to discuss ideas about the future, but had no idea how the process might work. Most of us had attended these type of "off-sites" before, and were pretty jaded that the exercise would produce anything of value. I am happy to say we were flat wrong.

The consultants explained to us that we were to participate in Scenario Planning. We would create four scenarios … four future worlds that might exist. It was up to us to create them. One might be a world of plenty, another dystopian, another highly regulated, and one where a new technology (hyper loop?) was better than ours.

Interestingly, we were told not to try to *predict* which world was most likely to appear. Our instructions were to focus on what we would do no matter which world won.

That's when the light went on. None of us thought we could predict the *correct* world. It made more sense that if we prepared for *all* of the worlds, we had the highest likelihood of creating the right products for the future.

The military used a similar exercise after the Vietnam War. They projected a world where they were involved in many small insurgencies, one where they deployed major forces to areas (like China), where we'd never really fought before, etc.

In every scenario they determined that *joint operations* between forces would be key. In Vietnam they'd had difficulties with communications between Navy, Marines, Air Force, and Army as they used disparate communications gear. Standardizing the gear would make it easier to harmonize operations, and they did just that.

So, if there's any secret to figuring out how to deal with disruption, it's this.

What should you do no matter what type of disruption you are facing?

Scenario planning can help you "see" into your future, and lots of consultants teach it now and facilitate strategic retreats on it.

My goal here is to do a book version of a strategic retreat to help you imagine different scenarios so you're prepared no matter what your future brings.

I've divided this process into three sections:

1. **Ready** – What do you need to do to your culture and team to prepare for change?

2. **Set** – What should you do to determine where to compete and what the new product will be?

3. **Go** – What can help you get that product out the door?

READY

THREAT ASSESSMENTS

> "I couldn't do that. Could you do that?
> How can they do that? Who are those guys?"
>
> —Butch Cassidy, *Butch Cassidy and the Sundance Kid*

Incumbent organizations tend to view disruption as a threat instead of saying, "How could we do that?"

They look at a startup that is dramatically simplifying their business model, or eliminating dealers or co-opting their assets, and simply put up their hands.

It certainly doesn't have to turn out this way.

Remember, if you're an incumbent, you have the factory, the supply chain, the distribution, the lab, and the brand!

These are assets that a startup would kill for.

As soon as you start thinking this way, you become more confident you "can do that!"

However, as an incumbent, you also have the bureaucracy, the procedures, the processes, and the complacency, which make it very hard for you to change.

The key is to take a chainsaw to the inefficient and time-consuming maze of your current structure.

We will talk in more detail about how to do that in our upcoming chapters including how to:

- Create fearlessness
- Don't play pinball
- Run marathons and sprints
- Get smart

One of the best ways to begin a threat assessment is to ask if you're taking risks.

RISKY BUSINESS

"There are risks and cost to action.
But they are far less than the long-range costs of inaction."

—President John F. Kennedy

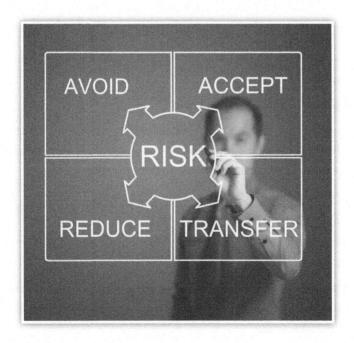

What do you do today when faced with risk? Do you avoid it?
Transfer it to someone else? Reduce it? Or accept it?

When we are talking about moving forward to avoid disruption you must accept some risk. Reduce it if you can, but accept it and move toward change.

Every company was founded by a risk taker. It is always a risk to start something new, I mean … you could fail. J

George Eastman at Kodak, Watson at IBM, Benihoff at Salesforce, Jobs at Apple, all took enormous risks to start products and companies that changed everything.

And yet as companies get older, they drive out risk. They have to meet the quarter, the street demands more, or they simply have to make payroll this week. There are lots of good reasons to take less risk. But as Kennedy says above, there are long-term costs.

Recently I was consulting on innovation with a large (over $150 mm) well-known charity. The discussion was going well and then they said, "What is the most important thing we can do to make us more innovative?"

"Take risks and be willing for some projects to fail," I replied.

There was dead silence on the phone.

"But we can't fail", someone finally blurted, "we have donors, they expect success."

I thought, "OK, we are in trouble here."

And then someone got it. "Hey, we've got lots of donors from Silicon Valley. They are used to failure, perhaps we could create a fund for innovation that they could donate into, and they'd be ok!"

Problem solved. Knowing that their leadership and donor base was risk averse, they found a group who wasn't.

Reduce the risk, find someone with courage to sponsor the risk, or just take the risk and ask forgiveness. But take the first risk!

I started my career as a receptionist in a travel agency almost fifty years ago. Six months into my first job my manager said, "Would you like to join me in a startup?"

I think he'd found a kindred spirit as he and I were both frustrated with our Luddite of a boss who didn't want to change anything.

You might think that was a big risk. Yet I was young, single, living in an apartment, and not making much money anyway. It was a small risk.

My new boss, Charles, was a Korean American. That didn't matter to me but as it turned out it mattered a lot to the Soviets. I found out that for years when they asked his heritage, he told them he was "Hawaiian" because the Soviets would not allow anyone born in South Korea come to the USSR.

Which is how, three months later, at the ripe young age of 22, I found myself in the USSR negotiating with a Soviet ministry to allow us to become only the fifth travel agency in the US that could make travel arrangements in Russia.

Charles took a chance on me and I returned home with the deal. I had been in way over my head but somehow swam my way to success. It certainly gave me confidence that helped as the company moved forward.

Over the next five years, we opened four offices (one in Moscow), became a multimillion-dollar agency, and entered the realm of the top fifty agents in the US.

Small risk. Nice reward.

When I look back at that period, it is hard to find just one thing that contributed to our success. But if I had to pick one, it was probably our adoption of technology.

Our first large client wanted us to produce sophisticated travel reports that their mainframe was doing for them inhouse. We had to find a way to do it "on the cheap" and we did using timesharing.

They wanted all reservations orders to come to us in writing so we got a fax machine, a real rarity at the time (about the size of a credenza!). We were an early adopter of in-house reservations terminals and mini-computers to produce itineraries and tickets. We were small, which meant we were nimble and could take risks other travel agents weren't willing or able to do.

All the computerization we had done at my first startup led me to the next. I moved to Agency DataSystems, a startup that sold mini-computers to travel agencies. I became fascinated in how computers were changing business. Because we were a small company, I got to sell them, install them, and train people how to use them. Eventually I got to lead the team that designed the software.

Small risk. Bigger reward.

Six months in that company was sold to American Airlines. Suddenly I was in a very large corporate environment (and the only employee among 50,000 in the marketing department with a beard!)

I began climbing the corporate ladder. I became director and then President of what was the Agency DataSystems division.

One day my boss said, "I'd like to make you VP of computer programming. You will have a team of 500 programmers."

"But," I protested, "I don't know anything about programming!"

"You'll do fine," he assured me.

He was right; I did fine and had a wonderful time learning how a history major and travel agent could help drive change and success with programmers.

A few years later a new boss called, "I want you to take over computer operations. You will have a team of 1,000 have a budget of $300 million and be responsible for the uptime of one of the largest computer systems in the world."

"But, Kathy, I don't know computer operations!"

"You'll do fine."

I did but it was a really tough job. Particularly difficult was *improving quality* and *reducing cost* while *increasing uptime*.

Two years later another boss called. "We are spinning off the SABRE division from American Airlines. I want to make you Chief Information Officer."

This time I didn't protest; I just happily accepted the promotion. I rode the ripple effect that results when you're willing to take wise risks.

In each case, the company basically dumped me in a totally new situation and watched my performance. I think they took the risk as there were already great teams below me and they wanted me to grow and adapt.

It was up to me to look at the department and the team and find out how I could propel the group forward.

What I discovered was that CIO was a great title, not a particularly great job. It was a coordination role with lots of responsibility for outcomes but with little ability to get into the weeds and get things done myself. I preferred to be challenged.

Which is why I decided to take a leap of faith and take a huge risk.

I was married, had two kids, a nice salary, and a big mortgage.

But I had spotted something that had great potential: our fledgling online department. I set a meeting with my boss and told him I wanted to quit being CIO and go run that little department.

"You're nuts," he said, "It's tiny. There are only 12 people in that department, you are managing thousands!"

"True," I replied, "but I think it is going to be big."

We turned that "little" online department into Travelocity and took it public for $1.2 billion.

The reason I felt confident to take that risk was that the previous twenty years had been an advanced course to run and scale a business. I'd been a travel agent, a product marketer, run IT, and been a CIO. I'd been in startups and a big company.

It was the perfect background to be CEO of an Internet startup. And since I'd managed both small and large operations, it prepared me for the stratospheric growth that Travelocity experienced.

If you have a chance in your career to move around and gain a variety of experience and expertise, do it! If you see potential that calls you, go for it.

The more you learn, the more valuable you become, the more ripple effect results you'll reap.

Big Risk = Big Reward

SABRE eventually decided to buy back Travelocity and take it private.

Once again, I decided it was time for me to try something new.

I launched a variety of projects. I became a professional speaker and spoke around the world to organizations like Cisco, Aflac, Harvard University, FedEx, Pfizer, Intel, and the International Shopping Center Association.

I started a small consulting operation and wrote a book.

I joined a venture capital firm to help them explore travel investments.

That's where the idea for Kayak.com was born. I served there as chairman for eight years. Along the way, there were many twists and turns and changes of business models.

But, as discussed, bumpy roads are the way of startups. There is no certainty and no expressway to success. But in the end, we took it public for $1.2 billion and a short time later sold it to Priceline for $1.8 billion.

Another risk I've taken? Serving on seventeen public and private boards. Some of these companies shrank, some disappeared entirely, and the rest created over $6 billion in value.

Again. Risk and reward.

You've heard of *The Tale of Two Cities* written by Charles Dickens? Well, this is the Tale of Two Startups.

- One that shrank was a dial up Internet access company. The broadband world rendered dial up useless. It was too slow – and frankly too late – to try to transform to a cell phone provider. It was sold for a fraction of its previous value.

- One that has had great success is Boingo. Formed as a Wi-Fi hotspot company it had found its niche as a Wi-Fi provider in airports around the world. It was a good business. Then airport visitors told airports that Wi-Fi should be free and things got really tough.

  But Boingo adapted quickly and promptly. They put Wi-Fi into every US Army, Air Force, and Marine base world-wide. They moved into providing cell service in airports and stadiums (where phone companies can't build towers) and into providing Wi-Fi and smart home services in multifamily housing (apartments).

Boingo owes its success to its willingness to constantly adopt new technologies and new business models *ahead* of their biggest market change. They were learning, adapting, and hedging their bets, all at the same time.

Five years ago I took another risk, I cofounded a travel-related AI company.

At age 65, did I have to do another startup? No, I'm on Medicare; I didn't *have* to do another startup. I *wanted* to do another startup.

We produced great software, and had terrific customers like Hilton, Marriott, Intercontinental Hotels, and Emirates Airlines. We won lots of awards. But try as we might we couldn't earn our keep. Selling to large corporations is complicated as you're dealing with layers of bureaucracy. Most of them, even though they saw good results, were risk-averse and weren't willing to bet on a startup.

Late last year we went bankrupt.

Am I disappointed? Sure. Yet 70% of venture-backed startups fail and less than 50% make it past their fourth birthday. I shrugged and put this in perspective. To have one failure out of five startups isn't a bad track record.

So, am I done taking risks?

No way. I've just had a $15-million-dollar advanced course in what not to do!

As Rich Gingras, VP of Google News, said, "There are no failures. We tried something and we learned something." (*MIT Sloan Management Review*)

You may be reluctant to disrupt your organization because you're afraid it will fail.

The irony is, your organization will fail if you do not disrupt it.

If you are not making mistakes along the way, you are not experimenting enough.

Take the first risk. It is the first step on your journey to avoid disruption.

CREATING FEARLESSNESS

"You fall? You die!"

—Karl Wallenda

The Great Wallendas were the world's best high-wire act for decades. They performed their tricks without a net. Unfortunately, several of them died.

Yet, like Evel Knievel, the motorcycle jumper; George Willig, who climbed the World Trade Center; and Fred Fugen, who base-jumped from the Burj Khalifa, they chose to live with the fear and for the thrill.

Wallenda's most famous quote is, "Life is on the wire. All the rest is just waiting."

Most people don't feel this way! They don't like putting themselves in danger and would rather not take risks. We've all met them in business.

Which is why managers have a responsibility to make risk-taking … safe.

And no, that's not an oxymoron.

In fact, Zappos founder Tony Hsieh has a mantra, "Is it safe enough to try?"

The easiest way to make everyone feel that it is safe enough to try is to adopt the motto "Kill projects, not people."

I explained this mindset in my book On Innovation, but it bears repeating here.

And the outcome, by the way, cannot be like the cartoon below.

Once at Travelocity I had a million-dollar project failure. Everyone had signed off on the plan, the product was well manufactured and had great distribution, but customers simply were not interested

I had to go to my boss (who at the time was the CFO at American Airlines and a real tough case) and explain I'd lost a million dollars.

His answer changed our culture. "*What did you learn?*" he said.

I wasn't punished. My career wasn't over. We used that moment to learn and to move on.

What was different is that he and I made sure that moment was very *public*. American had a very perfectionist culture at the time. And that made sense, for the operational side of the business. But not in areas of innovation.

By the way, we didn't have to try hard to make it public. The rumor mill was already going strong about the "million-dollar failure" and many people assumed it meant my demise (or at the least, a demotion). So when that "epic fail" was embraced instead of punished, it was like a tweet from a president: it got noticed.

By "going public" with that mistake, we emphasized that our culture had changed. It set a valuable precedent so other internal innovators wouldn't be risk-averse.

If a project fails, and the staff gets another chance, co-workers will notice. It gives them a safety net which makes them a lot more willing to risk a "high-wire" project.

Yes there are some people who just aren't willing to take risks. Just like there is a small group of people who buy flight insurance for every flight, even though the risks are much smaller than driving. Those folks don't belong on your disruption/innovation team.

As my GM at Travelocity used to say, "Negative people are energy vampires." It is so true. They drag down the team and kill confidence. Find them another place to hang out, and seek out those who understand risk-taking is not a path to career destruction. Those are the ones who will propel you – and your project – forward.

Key point: We are talking about a tolerance for *failure* not a tolerance for *incompetence*.

Learning from failure means looking for the lesson. What did we learn about:

- Our customers?

- Future trends?

- How we work together (right team?)?

- Our skills and talents?

I saw this fictional (but spot-on) quote somewhere (sorry, can't remember where):

"I want it done correctly, accurately, exactly, perfectly, reliably, flaw-lessly, and efficiently. I want it unharmed, unbotched, untainted, and most of all cheap."

Put this way, it looks crazy. Yet many managers give exactly that impression when they set a team out on their innovation voyage.

Please get this: if the team doesn't feel safe, they won't stretch themselves to take risks. And if they don't take risks, you won't get change or make progress.

As the saying goes, "You don't need a parachute to go skydiving. You need a parachute to go skydiving TWICE."

Supply your team with good working parachutes – and with the mental safety net that mistakes are to be learned from, not punished – and they will soar.

FIX THE ODDS

"Every now and then a trigger has to be pulled. Or not pulled.

It's hard to know which when you are in your pajamas."

-James Bond, *Skyfall*

Agreed. It is hard to know when to pull the trigger on a new product, which is why experimentation is so key to success.

The funny thing is, many companies experiment constantly in some areas of the business – but not in others.

Wannamaker's famous quote "50% of my advertising is wasted. Trouble is, I don't know which half" doesn't apply anymore.

With the rise of digital advertising and analytics, we know with perfect accuracy which ads work and which don't.

Marketing departments are constantly experimenting because they're tasked with creating a bottom-line competitive edge. In selling to new corporations I found marketing much more open to trying AI than IT was.

Science-based companies are built on experimentation. One of my clients is a large drug company. I didn't know much about that industry, but I certainly knew that developing a new drug required years of experimentation. So, I thought, this entire company must have a culture of experimentation. Boy, was I wrong!

As I worked with their digital department, we brainstormed new ideas and the excitement grew. But late in the day I began to hear, "We will never get sign off," "We've never done things like this," and "It's not in the budget."

Finally, we began to discuss where experiments fit in their culture and how they could sell "upper management" on being willing to try new things. Perhaps they didn't have to cross every t and dot every i. Perhaps they didn't have guarantee a profitable outcome to receive funding to test.

We landed on a strategy of praising their company's successful history and track record of experimentation, and pitched their plan like a new drug. It worked!

At Travelocity, we split our development team between "quick hits" and big projects as we realized the amount of our effort was not related to customer satisfaction.

"Quick hits" were things that we could produce in less than six weeks. We didn't require they be fully stress-tested and have all the kinks worked out, we just pushed them into the field and sometimes called them "beta." Not all of them worked out, but that was ok because some did. Quick hits were cheap to try and we learned a lot from this willingness to experiment and learn along the way.

Look at your business? Are there some "quick hit" projects or products where you could shorten delivery time to get new offerings out in the market that would delight your customers?

As the saying goes, "Beta isn't just for software anymore."

Another way to delight customers is with "quick hit" updates.

For example, Tesla has amazing customer satisfaction due to their ongoing updates.

I know I've used Tesla as an example several times in this book, it's just that they are a role model of how to turn customers into raving fans with constant iteration.

Sometimes I get a bug in the entertainment system or discover the new AI powered wipers are not perfect. But then, it will get fixed *and* when

I receive an update with a free dash cam or security system that makes up for everything.

Tesla customers voluntary sign up for beta tests because they see it as a perk. This is a win for all involved because Tesla receives constant feedback about what is not working so they can correct it. As a bonus, their customers feel listened to - which makes them strong brand proponents who eagerly tell everyone who will listen how much they love their car.

If you aren't in software, there are plenty of other ways to experiment. 3D print your prototype and show it to customers. Use social media to put new ideas out there and ask people what they think. Use online panels … the list goes on.

Malcolm Forbes said, "The way to a man's heart is through his … opinion."

Ask people for their opinion – and act on it – and they will be fans for life.

While I was at Kayak almost 20% of our pages were in test all the time. We were constantly testing, frequently failing, but continuously learning, and frequently adapting. That's a prescription for success.

If you want to succeed?

Get into the lab. Ask people what they think. Act on their advice.

CLOSE THE ROACH MOTEL™

"It is very difficult to get a man to understand something when his salary depends on him not understanding it."

—Upton Sinclair, Author

In the late 70s, insect control brand Black Flag invented a catchy slogan for its sticky roach killing system: "The Roach Motel. "The roaches check in; they never check out!"

Their slogan popped into my head when I was thinking about what it's like to propose new ideas in large corporations.

It may be a great idea, but when you share it … well, let's just say, it goes in and it never comes out.

"Where the hell did that come from?"

If you read a lot on innovation and disruption as I do, you often see the phrase "Burn the silos." It's a wonderful concept in theory; unfortunately it can be hard to do in reality.

Silos can be departments or divisions that are closed off, that focus on themselves, that don't share.

Silos are often bulwarks against idea adoption. They may be necessary in large organizations, but too often silos cause a NIH – Not Invented Here – mentality.

As Jeff Bezos puts it, "Even well-meaning gate keepers slow innovation."

For a time, I ran an organization called SABRE Labs. It was built as a technology incubator to foment ideas and plant the seeds for new products. We invented the mobile boarding pass long before any airline deployed this idea, but the idea was never deployed.

We proposed allowing customers to track lost bags over the Internet (no one did that till 20 years later!). Even though many of our ideas were visionary and could have made the company a lot of money and given us a competitive edge, few made it out of the lab.

Why? They were generally rejected out of hand as they didn't originate in the destination department. In other words, we got SILO'd.

Think about your organization.

- Are there silos where new ideas go in and never come out?
- Is the "Not Invented Here" syndrome rampant in your organization?
- Is it because your delivery muscle outpulls your discovery muscle?

It is possible to completely redesign an organization to eliminate existing silos, but it is such a radical investment of resources, it's quite rare. When done successfully though, it can generate impressive results.

For example, as explained in Gillian Tett's book *The Silo Effect*, the Cleveland Clinic decided to look at their organization from the *customer's* perspective rather than from a *medical* perspective. This prompted them to completely redesign their structure.

They collapsed the "medical" departments and "surgical" departments and instead created 'institutes' organized around diseases or body systems. They created the "Head and Neck Institute" and the "Heart and Vascular Institute" where cardiologists and heart surgeons worked side by side to solve the patients' issues.

"If someone has a headache, they just want to get it fixed," said Toby Cosgrove, CEO, "They don't know if they need a neurologist, neuroradiologist, or a whatever, so it makes sense to put them together."

As a result of blending "silos" Cleveland Clinic went from one of the lowest ranked hospitals to having the highest patient satisfaction in the US. It is highly ranked in the top three positions in terms of medical skill in most specialties.

Moving from a product centric organization to a customer centric one can produce bottom-line profits, as Intel and Dell who have adopted this model can attest.[24]

But that isn't the only way to shake up silos. Sometimes swapping executives is the answer.

Our VP at SABRE got tired of hearing our Operations director complain about the Sales Department and vice versa. One day he told the two executives leading these areas, "Effective immediately, John you are no longer running Ops. You are now running Sales. Jim, you are now running Ops."

The executives were stunned, as were their teams.

But the swap had exactly the effect the boss intended.

Both got busy. They dug in and eliminated many of the problems they'd been carping about. They also discovered first-hand that some of the problems were more challenging than anticipated. They understood, for the first time, that the only way to solve them was to collaborate, not to complain.

That working together part, as we've seen throughout this book, is key.

As Cosgrove said, "Innovation happens at the margins, where one discipline rubs up against another."

Another silo-busting maneuver is to consolidate a function under a single executive without changing all departments.

At Travelocity, (as mentioned briefly before) my VP of Marketing was constantly complaining about how the IT department managed our CRM system. He told me many times, "They are too slow and just don't understand what Marketing really needs. I could do it better."

I finally called his bluff and moved all the CRM programmers and analysts into Marketing. He could no longer complain that "those other guys" weren't listening, as they were now "his guys."

He also had to learn how to serve the rest of the organization better than IT as that had been his claim. Putting those folks together broke down the silos and produced markedly better results.

Travelocity was initially a small department the SABRE group, which itself resided in the American Airlines Marketing Department. It consisted solely of the product management team who designed and marketed the product. Programming, operations, and finance were all farmed out to their respective organizations.

When the group was given to me, I wanted to set it up like its own little company, like a startup. I moved the group offsite and obtained enough space for everyone who supported the product to move in together. It wasn't as easy as that sounds. Each function wanted to stay in its silo. It took months to get some departments to agree to send their staff over.

Even when that was accomplished some folks had to attend two staff meetings (ours and theirs) and their compensation was closely held in their respective silo.

After about a year I was finally able to get everyone in the same office and on the same incentive plan (ours). Now, they were motivated to make Travelocity win. Boy, did that make a difference.

As Safi Bahcall notes in *Loonshots*, "As teams and companies grow larger, the stakes in outcome decrease while the perks of rank increase ... they begin rejecting."

What are *Loonshots?* As defined in his book with that title, they are: "a neglected project, widely dismissed, its champion written off as unhinged."

If you want your company to be open to *loonshots,* be sure to embed incentive in the success of the product team working together to achieve results.

We've all seen the helmet clad reporter in a war zone sign off with, "Silvia Richards, embedded with the 82 Airborne" ... or something to that effect.

At American, we embedded IT staff in every department we served. Usually just one or two, but their job was to live with the customer. They attended the staff meetings, were in on product design, and were the customer's advocate to IT. They could translate marketing speak into ITspeak and vice versa.

These embedded employees were a great help in creating innovation at the edge and preventing ideas from being killed. And when they told their customers that something "could not be done" they were believed, unlike IT because they had become part of the silo team.

Sometimes, you can go around silos by combining data between areas.

For example, Mike Flowers working under data meister Mayor Mike Bloomberg combined data to reduce tenement fires by using data on mortgage defaults, building code violations, poverty indicators, and structure age.

When confronted with a problem of clogged sewers from cooking grease, they matched clogged sewers with data on restaurants that didn't have a contract from grease removal and kitchen fires. All data from disparate databases in different departments. The inspectors followed the map and convinced the violators that they could actually *make* money by selling the grease.[25]

President Obama created a similar group of Silicon Valley types who reported to the White House, but began showing up at agencies where the President had heard of "insurmountable" problems. These "embedded experts" were usually rejected at first but as soon as the agency head heard "The President is calling," they were welcomed into the fold and allowed to get to work.

It takes seasoned data interpreters to understand how data may be combined to blend or bust silos and produce a new outcome.

That is one reason data scientists are in such demand today. Certainly we need great engineers, but we also need embedded analysts who can blend business and data to create new outcomes.

For example, at Travelocity we took flight and fare data (which we already had) and snow depth data (which we had to find) to create a map that showed the lowest airfares to the deepest powder skiing. Customers and the press loved it.

That led to an ad that used real-time data to say, "Its 10 degrees below in Minneapolis today and its 75 degrees in Miami Beach. Which is only $300 away."

American's Weather Department was flight focused and at first rebuffed our request for weather data, but in time they got excited about the products they helped create.

- Do you have departments that constantly carp at each other? Perhaps it's worth swapping managers so they put themselves in the other's shoes?

- Do you have data hoarders who never share? Perhaps they should "get a call from the President" or have am embedded swat team go around the silo and combine its data anyway?

- Could you follow the example of the Cleveland Clinic and blend silos (departments and specialties) and organize them around customer needs?

Whether you switch managers, combine data, or completely redesign your organization to eliminate silos just be sure that when ideas go in, they come out and they come out … improved.

Or, as a famous lyric from Johnny Mercer puts it:

"You've got to accentuate the positive

Eliminate the negative

Latch on to the affirmative

Don't mess with Mr. In-Between."

LOSE THE LUDDITES

"Who the hell wants to hear actors talk?"

—Hank Warner, CEO, Warner Bros. Pictures

When presenting my disruption talk, I often ask the sponsoring organization if I can run a ten-minute video during the break and as audience members come back into the hall and take their seats.

It consists of one hundred quotes, half of which are like the one above,

- "X-rays will prove to be a hoax" —Lord Kelvin
- "The truth is no online database will every replace your daily newspaper." —Clifford Stoll
- "Google is not a real company, it is a house of cards" —Steve Ballmer, CEO, Microsoft

The other half are ones like these:

- "Our best ideas come from clerks and stock boys" —Sam Walton, Founder, Walmart
- "The best way to succeed is to double your failure rate." —Tom Watson, Founder, IBM
- "The secret of change is ... not in fighting the old but building the new." —Socrates

I mix the two because the former make them laugh, the latter give them hope.

But as Steve Jobs said, "You can't connect the dots looking forward, you can only connect them looking backwards. You have to trust the dots will somehow connect in your future."

It's easy to laugh looking back; looking forward can be more of a challenge.

There are lots of luddites out there who hang on to the past and are fearful of the future. These folks can really put the brakes on your efforts to change.

As my friend Tom Wheeler relates in his excellent book From Gutenberg to Google, when speaking about the introduction of the telegraph, "Messages delivered by "lightning" became fodder for pastors to frighten the faithful about how it could only be black magic, while the U.S. Post Office resisted its opportunity to adopt a technology faster than mail.

In addition to the garden variety luddites, there are corporate luddites whose job is to ensure your company avoids risk.

As mentioned, I've served on 17 boards of directors. All of them have audit committees (to avoid financial risk), some have cyber committees (to avoid hacking risk), and many have risk management committees.

None have innovation committees.

But wait! There's more! Reporting to the CEO is the Finance Department, the Security Department, and the Insurance Department … all working to avoid risk.

And then there is the quality assurance department, which doesn't like risk as it will probably introduce product defects.

A few years ago, I was asked to speak to ASQ, The American Society for Quality. I thought, "Wow. How am I going to talk about innovation here? These guys kill innovation unless it clearly improves the process with little or no risk."

I pondered for a while and decided to open with a discussion of brainstorming. I suggested that when considering new products, they have two choices. They can say "and" or they can stay mute. They'll get a chance to voice objections and figure out how to build quality and safety into the product later. In this initial stage of the process, they need to hold off on their objections.

I got some groans from the audience when I proposed this, but audience members admitted later they did have a tendency to shut conversations down because "change creates defects."

They agreed that if they wanted their company to thrive, they'd participate in the brainstorming process by saying "and" (instead of "but") so they stayed open to iteration. They could inject quality and safety issues into the discussion *after* options had been initiated and explored.

We've all heard examples of products that were turned down many times before they finally got approved. You're probably aware that the Xerox machine and the Post-It Note were initially rejected. But did you know that Ring, the video doorbell, was rejected on Shark Tank but later sold to Amazon for $1 billion?

Why does this happen over and over?

Even serious VCs who look at hundreds of startups and are supposed to know the signals of greatness can miss the next unicorn.

When commenting on how his firm missed joining the initial funding round for Airbnb, Mark Andreessen said, "We made the cardinal mistake of a VC, we viewed it through the lens of our current biases."

The "lens of our current biases" certainly drives many of us to see innovative opportunities as just another crazy idea.

There is another reason. In the beginning, new ideas aren't perfect. They are what Ed Catmull of Pixar dubs, "ugly babies."

He calls the early versions of Pixar movies, "truly ugly: awkward and unformed, vulnerable and incomplete."[26]

That is one reason new ideas are so easy to kill. They seem foolish – they "won't ever work."

Plus, if you are the one to kill them, you can quickly get back to working on the successful products that were created years ago and are currently creating revenue. That's why many of us are incented on the "now."

"In many ways the work of a critic is easy. We risk very little and yet enjoy a position over those who offer up their work and their selves for our judgment … But there are times when a critic truly risks something and that is in the discovery and defense of the new. The world is often unkind to new talent, new creations. The new needs friends." (Anton Ego, food critic in the movie *Ratatouille*).

One excellent way to avoid the "ugly baby" trap is to require leaders of new products to share their story of what their envisioned future will look like. Both Amazon and Cisco require this.

As we sat over coffee one day my friend John Rossman, author of *The Amazon Way* and a former Amazon exec explained how it works.

At Amazon, new product owners write a press release for a product *before they have begun to build it.* It focuses on the problem the product solves, a summary of the benefits, perhaps a quote from a hypothetical customer. It might include some drawings or a simple prototype. This release must be presented to management and defended to get a green light on the project. PowerPoint, is banned from these meetings.

It's a great way to get buy in from the team as people can "see" both the new product and their role in it.

Digital leaders are using these techniques and others to move quickly into this new world. McKinsey says that digital leaders are:

- 50% more likely to cut through bureaucracy
- 20% higher in willingness to challenge traditional approaches
- 29% more likely to test limits

Tom Jago of Last Drop Distillers invented Baileys Irish Cream (the world's best- selling liqueur) and many other famous brands. Looking back on his career, he said, "You have to be prepared for punches in the nose, that someone up the line will say, 'This will never work.' Don't take it personally. This isn't your child, this is an idea."[27]

True, Tom, although when we "birth" an idea, it can sometimes feel like a child and it hurts when someone calls it an "ugly baby." But as the saying goes, "Take criticism seriously, not personally."

Hopefully, with the techniques in this chapter, you can get luddites and naysayers on your side and focus on how your idea *can* work instead of why it *can't*.

DON'T PLAY PINBALL

"Faced with the choice between changing one's mind
and proving there is no reason to do so,
almost everyone gets busy on the proof."

—John Kenneth Galbraith, Economist

I talk to many corporations who are envious of the speed with which Silicon Valley startups make decisions. These nimble companies are constantly trying, failing, changing and moving on. Disruption is in their DNA.

Most larger corporations are not like that. They generally are deliberative, risk averse and ponderously slow. They focus on *delivery* more than *discovery.*

That approach might have worked in a time of limited disruption, but not today.

Consider that in the 18 months after the Google Maps App was introduced in 2009, as much as 85% of the market cap of the top standalone GPS makers evaporated.

Google maps was so ubiquitously available and so well put together that there was obviously no longer much of a market for standalone GPS

Decisions today need to be made with Silicon Valley speed. They try it, test it, and implement it. Or, they try something else.

In my speech on disruption I show audiences the Pinball Decision Machine which shows my model for how many corporate decisions are made:

Think of the pinball bumpers as departments. You introduce a new idea to the company and it generally works like this. First you hit the bumpers,

Bumper 1 – Manufacturing, "We could never make this"

Bumper 2 – IT, "Not our area of expertise"

Bumper 3 – Marketing/Sales, "No way we could sell that!"

Bumper 4 – Customer Service, "No idea how to service that"

Each time you trot out a new idea, you get bounced around until you finally end up in the gutter.

If you do manage to convince those departments this is actually a workable plan, you now have to navigate your idea through those flippers at the bottom of the game.

Flipper 1 – Finance

Flipper 2 – Legal

Those departments bounce your idea ball back and forth endlessly until it is eventually … GAME OVER!

The short video of this pinball machine management style usually generates gales of laughter, as the audience knows this is exactly how decision-making works in their organization.

After showing the video, I make my point. The combined intelligence and experience of your organization is greater than any startup in your field – *but only if you work together and leverage them to compete!*

Your mantra in the 21st century ought to be "Say yes to new ideas and take the risk."

The key to being open to new ideas is to agree to use the word "and" instead of the word "but."

That one simple change – becoming an "and" person rather than a "but" person – is the key to embracing and exploring ideas instead of dissing them from the outset.

The folks at Pixar call this "plussing." It's about adding-on, not subtracting which is a non-negotiable when dealing with risk-avoidant personalities.

One company told me recently they had discovered their purchasing division was a perpetual idea-killer. They consistently said no to every new idea. So the team pushing the new idea made a concerted effort to get purchasing on their team by convincing them that purchasing was key to the company's future success. By persuading these nay-sayers that their cooperation was the lynchpin of their future, and giving them loud credit for their active support, they turned a no vote into a yes.

Want a fun analogy?

You already know I like the game of pinball and use it as an analogy for what happens to ideas and decisions in many large organizations.

What you may not know is that I had an opportunity to play pinball on a ferry that took me across the inland sea of Japan.

It was a turbulent day with lots of whitecaps. At one point the rhythmic roll of the ship as it crested one wave after another caused the pinball to roll back and forth, back and forth, between the same two bumpers. Bing, bing, bing. Bing, bing, bing.

That one back-and-forth play racked up points for almost ten minutes (!) before the ferry shifted and the ball rolled into the gutter ... but not before generating the highest score I've ever gotten. That ship was "plussing" my score rather than shooting me down as a loser.

That's the kind of culture you want. A culture where each bumper (department) is saying "yes, and" over and over, iterating the idea and racking up high-scoring points instead of sending your idea prematurely into the gutter.

RUN MARATHONS AND SPRINTS

"You can run a sprint or run a marathon.
But you can't sprint a marathon."

—Ryan Holmes, CEO, HootSuite

A few years ago, I was asked to speak at a Gartner IT conference on "bi-modal IT." The concept was that in IT organizations there's pressure to keep everything running flawlessly always – and at the same time innovate and create new things.

In other words, you need to be "bi-modal" … do both at once. As you can imagine, doing both of those things at the same time can be a recipe for culture clash.

It is probably why the CEO of Panera Bread said that in many companies, "The delivery muscle overwhelms the discovery muscle. We get so good at delivery we don't want to take any risk of something new that might slow delivery."

I'd never heard the term "bi-modal" IT before that Gartner conference, but I'd done it intuitively.

At American Airlines, I was charged with running what was, at the time, one of the largest computer systems on the planet. We automated 40 airlines and 40,000 travel agents. The people we chose to perform that task were no-nonsense, quality-oriented operations types who were (with good reason) resistant to change.

And that is exactly what we wanted in that area. We purposely made it very difficult to change the operational core of the system because change = bugs = downtime.

I was running Travelocity at the same time I was in charge of the computer system. It was a different world at Travelocity. Our priority was to quickly turn ideas into code and get them out for customers to try.

We were in a separate building from those "operational types." We had such a different culture, we might as well have been on a different planet. We even separated our "quick hits" team from those who were building the infrastructure.

Our "bi-modal" mentality was a major reason we were so successful.

As mentioned earlier, Walmart made it possible for their large organization to move quickly by "doing the new" in a separate lab. BestBuy and REI initially created separate divisions for their web efforts so as not to disturb their core stores.

Steve Jobs famously moved the Macintosh division into a separate building so as not to be held back by the Apple II team. "It's better to be a pirate than to join the Navy," he said. He was emphasizing that his little startup division wasn't going to be held down by the corporate rulebook or the corporate culture. Sometimes you have to be a pirate to get things done.

I spent a lot of time on how to structure new ideas for success in my previous book, so I'll just briefly mention that in addition to moving to a separate building to become bi-modal at Travelocity we:

- Hired as many external people as internal

- Had a completely separate budget than our parent SABRE

- Had a totally separate organization that reported to the CEO

In SABRE operations, it was just the opposite. We used operational excellence tools to stamp out defects and perfect 99.9999% uptime.

It's important to clarify which culture is right for your division and which rules can be broken and which can't.

I'll never forget the computer operator who deliberately violated procedure (took a shortcut) and made American Airlines unable to price a ticket for 24 hours. That rogue computer operator put me in the unenviable position of having to explain to our Chairman at 3 a.m. that I had no idea when the system would come back up. His "little shortcut" cost us millions and I had to tell him he had no reason to come to work on Monday.

"But you told us it was ok to fail," an employee remarked at an all hands meeting held shortly thereafter.

"Yes," I said, "but it's not ok to violate procedure and crash the system. Experiments are great when there is a plan and we understand the risks. Flipping a switch to see what will happen is quite another thing."

Marathon runners and sprinters learn different skills, they train differently and they run dramatically different races.

Separating the marathon runners (your operational teams) and your sprinters (your innovation teams) is the key to moving forward while still making the quarter.

Now that we've reviewed how to "Get Ready," lets "Get Set" by talking about Godzilla, Magic Things, and Perpetual Motion!

GET SET

GODZILLA DIDN'T KILL KING KONG

"The best swordsman in the world doesn't
need to fear the second best swordsman in the world."

Mark Twain, Author

Twain goes on to say that the man to fear is the person who has never held the sword before because he "does the thing he ought not to do ... and catches the expert out and ends him on the spot."

It's the same with King Kong. Kong wasn't slain by another giant, but by a squadron of biplanes, that must have looked to him like mosquitos.

In this world of disruption, it's unlikely your largest competitor will be your undoing. The problem is those five to six thousand new startups per year that are attacking the traditional world.

You need to put their ideas to work and become a disruptor yourself.

CB Insights produces hundreds of market maps showing the start-ups disrupting industry. Here is a sample.

(source: CB Insights "Know your industries: 100 MarketMaps)

These are extremely useful and I'd encourage you to subscribe to their service (expensive) if you can or get their emails at minimum.

You can use these maps to get a sense of what is happening in your market.

As John Chambers says in his excellent book *Connecting the Dots*, "You compete against market transitions, not against other companies. If you don't stay focused on the market it doesn't matter if you win a few battles now and then."[28]

One way to do what Chambers suggests is to use market maps and look for trends.

Which areas are gaining funding? You can subscribe to VentureBeat to learn. Where do you feel most vulnerable? Look at the components of the market map and see what is going on in that vulnerable area.

Don't just have research look at what is happening with your top competitors. It's smart to focus on startups and trends as well. As Bill Clinton said, "Focus on the trendlines not the headlines." That is spot on for incumbents.

Another way to look for trends is to spend time on the edges of the biggest trade show in your industry.

As a speaker I always stop by the trade show before I give my speech. It gives me a pulse of what's hot … usually in the largest booth.

But I also take time to patrol the edges … the tiny booths, because that is where the breakthroughs are likely to be. Just because they don't have the biggest booth and the best tchotchkes doesn't mean they don't have the coolest new product.

Years ago, I was circling the edges of the largest computer show in the world when I stumbled upon an amazing printer. Its printouts looked just like a typeset page and it was sized to fit on a desk. Most printers of that era were those noisy dot matrix jobs that produced very odd text.

I asked the lonely fellow in the booth what it was. "Laser Printer," he said in halting English, "First desktop sized." I asked if I could buy it. "No, only one we made."

You never know what you will find! And this one set me on a quest to see how we could print better flight itineraries for our customers.

Another way to follow trends is to visit what's called "The Silicon Valley Petting Zoo." This simply means take a trip to Silicon Valley and arrange for a VC to set up a day for you to visit startups in your industry. (Andreessen Horowitz hosts many of these.) Believe me, it's an eye-opening experience to see these hungry companies with their bright entrepreneurs all focused on creating the next big thing.

I quoted Ken Chenault, the former Chairman of American Express, in the introduction to this book. That quote came from a dinner I attended with him and the executives of a dozen startups in Menlo Park.

Chenault made it a habit to go there two or three times a year with his top team to take the pulse of change. He clearly knew that Fintech was real, that it was a threat he needed to be on top of, and found a brilliant way to do just that.

Comcast has worked with over 1500 startup leaders to understand the best way to interact with them. They spend lots of time at it and it has resulted in raft of proof of concepts and several profitable contracts.

The Director of Technology Accelerators for the Air Force is Captain Steve Lauer. He makes a very good point about how to engage with start-ups in a report from Innovation Leader. He says almost everyone tends to see a problem and then describe the solution they want, rather than simply ask for a solution.

"If we want to see over a hill for whatever military purpose, what we have a tendency to do is to say, 'Look, I need you guys to create me a satellite that's going to be in geo orbit. It's going to have these specifications.' Very specific, and, in reality, we just wanted to see over the hill. We don't care if they come back with a hot air balloon or a carrier pigeon with a camera on it."[29]

I have an author friend who discovered the same thing. She asked her son (who works in Mission Control at Johnson Space Center) to help her work with a freelancer who was producing the cover of her next book. Her son Tom looked at her step-by-step instructions and laughed, "You'll get a terrible cover if you send that. It's way too detailed."

She asked why. He explained that flight controllers working with the International Space Station send what's called a "requirement document" to astronauts. It bullets end results but does *not* indicate the process to get the results. As Tom told her, "It would be an insult to an astronaut's intelligence to tell him/her what to do."

She got it. The freelancer was the expert, not her. If she wanted to tap into his and creativity and come up with a cover that was better than she knew how to produce, she had to give him the freedom to contribute his own know-how.

How can you apply that insight to your company? Perhaps by asking startups how they would solve issues and listening to their fresh perspective with an open mind.

How else can you tap into the disruptive DNA of startups?

Have you thought of corporate venture capital? There are over 200 corporate VC arms investing in startups today (CB Insights Corporate VC Report).

Interestingly, 80% say they do so to strategically align with emerging companies, but surprisingly 76% also say they are looking for financial returns.

Having served as a director on seven public company boards, I'd say I'm all for number one and skeptical of number two, as so few startups make it. There are some other great reasons to invest though. 47% say it helps them be a thought leader in the category, and 28% say they get early relationships with potential acquisition targets.

In corporate VC investments I believe it is key to make sure that the corporation actually believes in and uses the product.

Not all corporate VCs require this, but if your firm is going to potentially buy the startup, then up-front utilization of the startup's product is a must.

I've had two experiences where corporate VCs wanted to invest in one of my companies, but the relevant department wouldn't use our product. I needed the money at the time, but in the end I'm glad they didn't invest, as that refusal to use our product was a red flag warning.

If you determine from the research laid out above what is about to happen in your industry you have several choices.

- You could acquire a startup and use it to help change your mother ship. Just be careful not to kill it. Startups are fragile things and are also likely to upset the apple cart. When I was working with Aflac, I visited a startup they'd purchased to help them evolve. It had grown up in a city far away from headquarters and they were careful to keep it there. It's a smart idea as the startup would not have flourished inside the mother ship.

  American Airlines used a similar idea when they bought that little computer company where I worked. Bob Crandall, then the Senior VP of Marketing came down after the acquisition and said to us, "I am only sending one AA guy down here. A controller, to look after our money. Other than him I'm banning any AA employee from coming here for at least one year. If they come, they will kill you. Not out of malice, but they will lay on so much bureaucracy you will smother!" Two years later he deemed us 'grown up' and moved us to headquarters, where we did very well.

- You could wait until the startup becomes a grownup and buy it then for much more money. In this way you can be sure you've guessed right, but by waiting you may miss out. And acquisitions are difficult. Chambers bought and integrated over 150 companies into Cisco. One third of those acquisitions failed … yet that is the best record of any tech company. He emphasizes, "If your target doesn't share your values it doesn't belong in your family no matter how good the financials."[30]

- You could simply be inspired by what they have done and go home and try to do the same thing. Depending on your culture that could be simple or very difficult.

Walmart is an example of all these strategies. They joined the web early in 1996 but their website was clunky and had few products. I knew several of their CIOs and they were some of the savviest people I've met, but they even they couldn't seem to get Walmart on the right ecommerce path.

Walmart bought Silicon Valley companies and hired Silicon Valley execs, but like a virus they seemed to be surrounded by white cells and killed. A Bloomberg article from 2011 notes that store managers even fought against putting the website URL on shopping bags as it threatened their in-store sales.

Walmart has finally doubled down on ecommerce. It has paid billions to acquire companies like Jet.com and Bonobos, fought back on free shipping and finally begun leveraging its vast store network to its advantage. It has built a huge lab in Silicon Valley where it is creating stealth startups and houses tech acquisitions in areas like search, predictive analytics, and social shopping.

Although its ecommerce efforts pale in comparison to Amazon's, Walmart is now the 4th largest e-retailer and its ecommerce business grew 30% last year.

It has taken Walmart almost 23 YEARS to begin to get it right.

If you know Walmart this is not surprising. They have a very strong culture and almost all their senior managers started in the stores. So, that is where their heart is! It took several false starts, a determined CEO and even then a separate strong effort in Silicon Valley to get to #4.

Still by moving at a glacial pace to get to ecommerce, Walmart (2018 sales of $500 bbl) allowed Amazon's sales to grow to over $200 bbl.

I suspect Amazon feels somewhat like the guy in this cartoon at the prospect of Wallmart's online efforts.

So, what's the point of all this? Change can be hard. Knowing the right direction to change can be even harder.

But by visiting startups and by being open to new business models and technologies, you can increase the likelihood you'll be around for the next ten or twenty years.

"Those who predict the future we call futurists. Those who know when the future will happen we call billionaires." —Horace Dediu, Financial Analyst

If you can't predict the future, perhaps you can connect with experts and tap into their knowledge and vision. As with the freelancer and the Air Force Captain, don't tell these experts what you think, ask what they think and then listen and learn.

MAGIC THINGS

"The world is full of magic things, patiently waiting
for our senses to grow sharper."

—W.B. Yeats, Poet

In many discussions about disruption I've had with corporations people say, "We need an idea that will change everything."

But do you really need to invent fire or reinvent the wheel to be a disruptor?

Perhaps disruption is as simple as eliminating a customer pain point.

I've explained how Travelocity evolved out of EAASY SABRE, and that we created an online reservation product that we tested for years on early online networks like AOL. A few hundred thousand people used that product, and they told us that booking online was much easier than doing it over the phone.

That experiment became Travelocity. It started a revolution and today less than 7% of US travelers book airline tickets by phone.

Please note: Travelocity only changed *one thing* about booking travel. We made it self-service. In every other way we operated the same as agents. We used the airline systems to book, we issued (in the beginning) paper tickets, and we were licensed travel agents.

Kayak also changed *one thing*. As explained previously, Kayak began with a discussion of customer pain. At a dinner with the former executives from Expedia, Orbitz and Travelocity we discussed the fact that although we had millions of visitors to our sites, only about 5% actually made reservations. Our research showed that most actually did end up booking a trip, but they preferred to search with us and buy from the supplier directly.

So we said, "Let's provide choice and let people book where they want rather than be travel agents ourselves." At Kayak you can see everyone's price and then choose to book at Marriott or Expedia, for example.

Our one thing was *choice*, yet we created a company that sold for $1.8 billion.

Uber didn't change everything about personal transportation. In their first iteration the limos you rode in were most of the time driving for Cary Limo or Boston Coach.

What Uber did was change the user interface and made it very easy to get a ride. (To be fair, they had a new business model as well, but from a customer perspective they changed one thing – *the interface*.)

A company where I was a board member recently sold for $50 million. All they did was bundle attraction tickets together to they could be sold at a discount.

With SmartDestinations you could spend three days in Boston and use one ticket to get into the JFK Museum, take the Duck Tour, tour the Freedom Trail, etc. We were one of the first to offer online attraction bookings and by bundling we provided a price incentive to do so while at the same time providing incremental customers to attractions. Our one thing was *bundling*.

I mentioned Chiam Pikarsky earlier; he is known as "The Amazon Whisperer" because he has created thousands of products by reading Amazon reviews to discover what people don't like about a particular product and then producing a new one that eliminates that pain point! [31] His *one thing* is fixing what people don't like.

Every good pitch I review from a startup starts with "The Problem." They define the problem with the current way something is built or marketed and present how their new idea will fix that so we all get rich. If the idea gets funded, they proceed to try and disrupt incumbents.

Steve Jobs said, "Creativity is just connecting things."

True but perhaps industrial creativity is more than connecting things. It is connecting things in a new way that eliminates pain points.

Have you ever written a startup pitch for your product or organization? If you did, would you create exactly what you are selling now or would you pitch a new, faster, cheaper, more efficient version?

If you don't eliminate pain points in your product or service, some disruptor will do it for you.

As the adage goes, "The world's best candle makers continuously improved the candle. They didn't invent the light bulb."

Ask yourself and your team, "Are we improving candles or inventing light bulbs?"

I suggest you do both.

THERE IS NO PERPETUAL MOTION

"What prevents perpetual motion, Leonardo realized, is the
inevitable loss of momentum in a system
when it rubs against reality."

—Walter Isaacson, *Leonardo da Vinci*

Lots of systems today are rubbing against reality.

As noted earlier sometimes I look at a product or service and say, "That company is a zombie. They are dead but they don't know it."

I think that about my power company that is fighting a losing battle against solar power. I have a "smart electric meter" but I've yet to figure out how it benefits me.

I can't hook into my IOT devices to shift my power use to off peak, I can't look at it online to see my usage, it doesn't tell me what "phantom loads" (like TVs) are sucking power when off. Seems like a "dumb meter" to me.

Remember Ed and his limo company that I described earlier in the book?

The future was staring Ed in the face but he was paralyzed. His unwillingness to embrace disruption – him choosing to stay entrenched – doomed him and his employees.

There is no question that it is hard to change your business model, yet there are many examples of those that have.

- Netflix is the most popular example, moving from rental to streaming. It was painful and for a time crushed their stock, but they bet big and won.

- Western Union (are they still around?) successfully moved from sending telegrams to sending money. They are now the largest money transfer company on earth.

- Adobe now earns 45% of its revenue via digital marketing of content.

You may be familiar with the Buckminster Fuller quote, "There is nothing in a caterpillar that tells you it's going to be a butterfly."

You may not have heard the quote from George Westerman, the Principal Research Scientist at MIT Sloan who said, "When digital transformation is done right, it's like a caterpillar turning into a butterfly. But when done wrong, all you have is a really fast caterpillar."

So the question is, are you going to be a butterfly or a really fast caterpillar?

The limo company could have been a butterfly. They could have easily beta-tested a new online model with little risk or cost. Yet they stuck with what they knew rather than experimenting with the new.

Sometimes transformation is hard because not everyone likes the new idea. Netflix's CEO Reed Hastings said he finally had to remove the executives in charge of the DVD mailing business from team meetings as they kept trying to hold the streaming business back.

At Travelocity the rumblings from competing divisions about how much money we were taking "from them" to build our business eventually morphed into a chorus of calls for SABRE to sell Travelocity.

My boss brought all the executives together and held a formal debate on whether we should sell or keep Travelocity. (I was not allowed to speak.) We probably could have gotten a few hundred million if we'd sold it then. Thankfully the proposal to keep the company won the day and we later took the company public and SABRE's stake was worth over $800 million.

The best part of the debate was that it shut down further carping. By getting all the issues out on the table, we were able to move forward together.

How about you? Is there rumbling in your company about a new course of action? Could you get everyone together (with the CEO) to air your differences and reinforce the right course? If not, how will this caterpillar ever have a chance to morph into what it could be?

Perhaps the best way to begin your change may be with a simple assessment of your capabilities.

As Lars Sorenson, the CEO of drug giant Novo Nordisk (a client), put it:

- What are our strengths?
- What are our capabilities?
- What risks do we dare to take?

And as you've heard I believe the risk part is all important, or you won't apply your strengths and capabilities in new ways.

Remember you don't have to go "all in," maybe the best course of action is to simply move to something adjacent.

Komatsu, the massive construction machinery company (revenues of $22 billion) has its bulldozers used worldwide on construction sites. Rather than simply selling the bulldozers they now sell "dirt removal."

For Japanese customers they measure the job site with drones (reducing mapping time from two weeks to thirty minutes) and then their self-driving machines remove the dirt.[32]

Komatsu must have said to itself, "Our machines remove dirt, why shouldn't we?"

Standard Industries (the owners of GAF) is the largest roofing company in the world. They've just launched GAF Energy, which is all about solar rooftops. With 5 million homes getting re-roofed each year, but only 300,000 getting solar, there seems a large market opportunity.

Working with their existing dealers and making the installation simple and fast, they hope to increase total revenue substantially.[33]

They are also helping with permitting and financing. Will they eventually sell an outcome – power?

"We are already on the roof, what else can we do?" seems to be their motto.

Koch Industries is the second largest private company in the US with revenues of $110 billion. They are in over a dozen sectors and own a multitude of companies.

In his book *Good Profit*, Koch discusses what managing such a disparate group of companies entails. "In our experience a company tends to be better served when it is capability focused rather than industry focused."[34]

Georgia-Pacific is a Koch division who moved from selling paper towels for bathrooms to imagining how IOT could let them create a dispenser that would tell them when it was out of towels. That took them to selling touchless towel dispensers. Then they moved into selling touchless soap dispensers and then to systems that made sure hospital workers washed their hands.

They moved their focus from the purchaser of the towels to the user of the towel and thought how they could improve their experience. Then they used their *distribution capability and relationships to* sell more into the same space.

- How can you take your capabilities and leverage them to expand and digitize your products?

- What roof are you on and what else could you be doing up there?

- Do you sell products that "remove dirt" like Komatsu? Could you sell your own version of "dirt removal?"

GO!

PLACE YOUR BETS

> "When something is important enough, you do it
> even if the odds are not in your favor."
>
> —Elon Musk, CEO Tesla & SpaceX

Making bold bets is something venture capitalists do all the time. But VCs are simply in a different game than large companies. They know up front that 7 or 8 out of 10 of their companies will fail. But they play a long game and some become fabulously successful.

In a public company with all the pressure of activist investors, quarterly earnings and regulators breathing down your neck, the view is different. It is certainly easier to be conservative and make the quarter than to make a big bet.

Starting Travelocity was a big internal corporate bet. Don't forget when Travelocity launched, it was owned by American Airlines and the majority of their ticket sales came from travel agents. And Travelocity was in American's SABRE division and 100% of SABRE's customers were travel agents.

And yet, we decided to open a new business that was consumer direct and a direct competitor to our most important customers. This was over twenty years ago but from the Chairman on down, we were convinced that this was the future of airline ticket sales and so we placed the bet.

In a world of disruption, the winners are the ones who are willing to make a bold bet on the future.

As an article in *MIT Management Review* pointed out that in many markets, "Digital entrants [are] ... depleting revenue per yield per unit sold [of the competition] by 2% per year."

While this might not seem too painful, they also point out that, "With a profit rate of 10%, a 2% drop represents a 20% reduction in profitability." Ouch.

Bold bets set the stage for making the type of cultural changes that must occur when you are going to change the "way we've always done it."

The Boys in the Boat is Daniel James Brown's wonderful tale of the improbable crew team that won the 1936 Olympics. In it you read, "It isn't enough for the muscles of a crew to work in unison, their hearts and minds must also be as one."[35]

Product visions like Steve Jobs' vision for the iPod, "1,000 songs in your pocket" help bring the hearts and minds of the team in alignment.

It was something everyone could envision. Instead of stacks of CDs or a radio that always played what you didn't want to hear, it was all my music in my pocket!

It reminds me of an early vision at the Coca Cola Company, "A coke within hands reach of everyone in the world." Wow, every person in the company could internalize that message and understand how their actions could contribute to it.

How can you inspire people's heart and help them see a meaningful vision that motivates them to take action toward the end result?

For example, Martin Luther King didn't say, "I have a plan." He said, "I have a dream!"

Kennedy's vision was to "...land a man on the moon and return him to Earth." His visceral and visual "Moonshot" challenged and changed technology and gave US citizens something in common to work for and be proud of.

If you're thinking you run – or work for – a traditional company that doesn't like to "make or take bets," look at what's happening to traditional companies who are:

- The *New York Times* bet is to double its digital revenue in 5 years.
- Nordstrom is betting $14 billion in capital to improve its multichannel experience.
- GM is betting on an all-electric future: "Zero emissions, Zero accidents, Zero congestion."

GM CEO Mary Barra's mantra of "Zero emissions, Zero accidents, Zero congestion" is an example of a big bet that is easily understandable by her 170,000 employees. Everyone can understand their part in winning that race.

As mentioned, you don't have to bet the farm and go "all in." If you're playing a long game, you'll need to place many bets. And inside your bold bets, there should be many small strategic bets. (Since I live in Nevada, I enjoy gambling analogies.)

As Paul Clarke the CEO of Ocado puts it, "You have to make bets across many time horizons."

Bold bets can energize your organization. The question is, how can you keep change aligned and empower departments to change when they are all part of a process that produces the end product? One way is to follow the example of Haier.

Haier is the world's largest appliance maker with 75,000 employees. They have a radical approach to coordinating development. They have over 4,000 "micro enterprises," 200 are "transforming" MEs assigned to transform traditional businesses and markets, 50 are "incubating" ME's that work on emerging markets, and 3,800 are "node" MEs that provide services to the others like legal, accounting, design etc.

In this model the MEs decide whether to buy services from the open market or from the node MEs, forcing the nodes to become market based in their actions and pricing.[36]

To me, the Haier organization looks like the interior of an old pocket watch where some gears move slowly and some move at blurring speed. The customer-facing gears get to spin fast but they still rely on the larger and slower ones. It's a difficult model for most to achieve, but it has proven its benefits as Haier is growing gross profits at 23% per year.

You may now agree that it's important to place bold bets. You just want to know how to place the *right* bets.

One way to is employ agile teams.

Another way is to follow Toyota founder Sakichi Toyoda's advice. He suggested that before placing any bet or making any major decision, you "ask WHY five times!"

You'll learn more about how to do both in our next two chapters.

FASTER THAN A SPEEDING BULLET

"Faster than a speeding bullet, more powerful than a locomotive, able to leap tall buildings in single bound … Its Superman!"

—TV Intro to Superman, 1951

I wrote that quote from memory, as it was so impactful to me at a very young age.

Though Superman still hasn't arrived in the flesh (at least that we know of), the need to move "faster than a speeding bullet" is here now.

As we've seen, change is happening almost overnight. Think again about 90% of hearing aid production moving to 3D printing in only four years!

That's why so many companies are adopting "agile" organizational frameworks.

When I first heard about agile programming, it immediately made sense. I'd led huge mainframe teams that required giant binders of specifications, moved to PC teams that were smaller and moved faster, to the small web teams at Travelocity that tried to move at web speed.

But agile seems just the ticket for the pace of development today.

What is surprising is that for the first time in my memory, a method of organizing software development has moved into organizing large portions of major corporations.

Teams have been around forever, so what's different here?

To me, agile teams are like sports teams. When I think of the Boston Red Sox, I think about the players on the field and the coaches. I don't think about the GM, accounting and marketing department, and HR groups that support them. The team plays the game, the other groups are just support.

Agile teams are small. Members cut across disciplines. They are generally free to act and decide and are self-governing, but are accountable for outcomes. They are customer focused and use rapid prototyping and fast feedback loops.

Agile teams "almost always result in … faster time to market, better quality and lower risk than traditional approaches can achieve." —Riley and Noble of Bain in HBR.

And very large companies are adopting agile. SAP has over 2,000 teams; USAA, 500; and 3M, over 100. They are not just for new products anymore but are attacking all types of processing from "change of address" to the processes in delivering SAAB's new fighter jet.

As we noted before, when fast moving teams (sprinters) have to interact with slow moving bureaucracies (marathoners) … sparks fly..

At Travelocity, my key role was to provide air cover for the team and knock down the barriers created by the corporate groups (finance, purchasing, IT) that we had to interface with.

When we started Travelocity for business at SABRE, we used agile teams before they even had a name.

We selected innovative team members, made sure they had all the core expertise they needed in product management, programming, UI design, and clear interfaces to those things they didn't need too much of: finance, legal, purchasing etc.

We got them an apartment for an office and sent them offsite. They had a clear mandate and a short time frame and the authority to make decisions. And they built a business in very short order.

Today's agile is much like the teams we had, but today there is a trove of literature and advice to help you map your way to success in deploying it.

Two things to remember.

- You need agile to move at the speed required to avoid disruption

- Remember the little gear that spins fast (the agile team) and the big gears that move slowly (the support organizations) in the pocket watch analogy we spoke of earlier? It takes both to make the watch tell time. The trick is you have to oil the mechanism.

ASK WHY

"Why do we have to wait for the picture, Daddy?"

—Jennifer Land

That question was asked by the daughter of the future Polaroid CEO Edwin Land'. He must have answered something to the effect of, "Well honey, the film has to go to the store and be sent away to be developed and then they make the pictures they send back to us."

She thought about it for a moment and then asked, "But why do we have to wait?"

Jennifer's question forced Land to ask himself the same question. And that set him on a quest to "eliminate the wait." A multibillion-dollar instant photo company was the result.

I was trained in the Toyota approach of asking "WHY?" five times before making decisions – and taught how to use Ishikawa (or fishbone) diagrams – while at American Airlines. The questions and diagrams can help you get to the root cause of a problem. They are great tools to improve quality and spot defects in production.

Yet many companies who use the process don't use it to look at their core business.

It can yield some interesting results when you ask, "Why have we always done it this way?" not just once, but multiple times. Each question takes you deeper into traditional policies, procedures and rationales that may no longer be effective.

When I was running Travelocity, customers kept complaining they could not find the $99 flight they saw in a TV ad as you could not search for flights by price.

I asked my pricing programmers WHY this was.

"Well," they said, "the files of prices are linked to each flight on a particular day. You have to know the flight and day first, that's how pricing works."

But WHY?

I had to ask WHY five times to drill down to the cause of the problem to correct it.

1. "WHY can't I ask for a price and find a flight?"

   "Because fares are linked to flights."

2. "WHY are the prices only found linked to a particular flight?"

   "That's the way we built it."

3. "WHY?"

   "Because when we built it all flights between two cities had the same price regardless of date"

4. "WHY?'

   "Because the government regulated fares and all airlines charged the same price. So no one wanted to know which flight had which price. They all had the same one"

5. "So WHY can't we do it different way today?"

It actually took many more WHYs, six months, and a million dollars to redevelop the system but it was what we needed to do to fix the problem.

As a result of our WHY perseverance, we were able to create "Fare Driven Availability" and a fare calendar where you could click on a price and find a flight. Now every airline has it.

Elon Musk recently founded "The Boring Company," a company whose goal is to burrow under cities creating tunnels where vehicles can bypass traffic and get from A to B in minutes rather than hours. Once again it is a company working to relieve a customer pain point, i.e. sitting in LA traffic for hours to move just a few miles.

Digging tunnels is a long and laborious business. I know something about how hard this is as I lead the team that developed the reservations software for the Channel Tunnel between France and the UK and we certainly learned about digging delays and cost overruns as we couldn't get paid until the tunnel was working. The Chunnel was a year late and had 80% cost overruns. By comparison building the software was easy, though moving one hundred Texans to France for three years was not. ☺

Musk uses what he calls "First Principles Thinking" to challenge the way things are done today. He tries, he says, "to get to the physics of things."

In starting the Boring Company, he visited the manufacturers of those very large tunnel-boring machines that dig the tunnels.

Getting quickly to the heart of the matter as to why it took so long to dig he asked the engineers, "Are these machines thermally limited or energy limited?" (i.e., will they melt if they go faster? Or are they slow because they don't have more energy?) The engineers didn't know.

Musk's team determined that right now they are energy limited. So, they're increasing motor size and speed to increase boring speed 10×.

Similarly, when working at Tesla, he questioned battery costs. Historically batteries cost about $600 per KW hour. But by looking at the material costs he found that those costs were only about $80 per KW hour. By continually asking WHY and WHY NOT? they found a new and creative way to combine the materials into a battery.

One of the first principles is to create an audacious goal.

SpaceX started with the goal of colonizing mars and a step along the way led to reusable rockets, which of course everyone said could not be done. (If you haven't already done this, please go on YouTube and watch the SpaceX rockets return and land. I guarantee you will clap!)

I have no doubt that First Principles Thinking will help Musk achieve his goal, which is, "I want to die on Mars. *Just not on impact!*"

I talked to a rural bank recently whose goal was to make sure no transaction lasted longer than five minutes.

"WHY five minutes?" I asked.

The answer was fascinating. "Because that is generally how long it takes for a farmer to get from one end of the field to another in his tractor and all our customers do banking from their Internet connected tractors. They want to finish before they have to turn the vehicle at the end of the row!"

They had to ask many "WHYs" to reduce all their transaction times to five minutes. But having an audacious goal was the beginning to them disrupting their norm.

Customers want speed and convenience. If your company has been around awhile, chances are it is neither fast nor convenient.

Time to start asking your five WHYs. You might want to start with these at your next staff meeting.

1. "Why do we have to wait?"

2. "Why can't we do it faster?"

3. "What can't we do it less expensively?"

4. "Why have we always done it this way?"

5. "Why not ask our customers what they want?"

START UP YOUR ENGINES

"If everything seems under control,
you aren't going fast enough."

—Mario Andretti, Formula 1 Champion

My son has been in the video game business since he was in high school. He has worked for some of the biggest game companies: Valve, Sony, and Electronic Arts.

As mentioned earlier, in this book, a few years ago, he bet on himself. He quit working for the "big boys" and formed his own company with three other game developers.

How can four guys compete with companies like EA or Sony who regularly spend over $100 million on a game?

They use startup tools.

By that I mean that his game was:

- Funded on Kickstarter
- Their offices were in each guy's apartments (they used Slack and Skype to work together)
- They crowdsourced things they couldn't do themselves
- Some art design
  - All the music

- Legal

- Much of the marketing

- They used Amazon AWS for their infrastructure

- Their marketing was social media – no barrier to entry and free

Can your company use some of these startup tools to speed yourself along?

Did you know multibillion-dollar company Shell uses a Kickstarter knockoff internally to fund internal startups?

They have a team that you can contact if your new idea got shot down by your department head. They will put it up on the internal Kickstarter and just like public Kickstarter people can "donate" funds to get the project off the ground and reap the benefit when/if it works.

More and more companies are figuring out they can save money and expedite results by crowdsourcing services they don't have or that are cheaper than their internal sources.

Funny story. When General Dynamics experimented with crowd-sourcing some projects, they found almost half of the good ideas that were submitted were from their own employees! (They just hadn't been listening before.)

Perhaps this is a new way to get around the "roach motel" – where ideas go in and never come out – and break down silos.

The web is filled with lists of tools and products that startups use to move faster. Many are free, cheap, and easy to try.

For example, you might want to check out Amazon AWS for cheaper computer services, MailChimp for email processing, Google Docs, and Slack for collaboration, Github for development. The lists on Google go on and on.

The other day I got a call from a guy who wanted to talk to me about how Boingo was deploying IOT, he wanted to learn from our experience. What was interesting was that he introduced himself as an EIR (or Entrepreneur in Residence) as Shell.

Now, EIRs are a staple at venture capital companies. VCs recruit founders who have had a successful exit and have them work at the firm looking at new ideas or incubating them to create a new startup. Shell is doing the same thing! This EIR was charged to use IOT to create a new product not only for Shell but for the entire industry and Shell would incubate and invest in it. Talk about grabbing on to a startup tool. Good for them!

Utilizing these tools can get your team off the starting blocks quickly rather than waiting for central corporate resources to get around to helping you.

As Enzo Ferrari said, "Aerodynamics are for people who can't build engines."

Enzo means that if you have enough horsepower you don't have to spend your time optimizing your solution, you can just go fast!

And that is what thinking like a startup and using startup tools can let you do ... quickly.

"In the digital age of 'overnight' success stories such as Facebook, the hard slog is easily overlooked.", said Sir James Dyson of Vacuum fame.

Agreed, however if you're smart you can speed up the "hard slog" by playing like a startup.

GET SMART

"I'm a sportsman. I'll let you choose how you die!"

—KAOS Agent

"How about old age?"

—Maxwell Smart From the
TV show *Get Smart*

If you think about it, smart products are the best way for your products to "die from old age" rather than be killed by a disruptor.

Smart products have a real opportunity to protect you from upstream data collectors who could make your product the tail on the dog. They can also move you into new recurring revenue models like subscriptions by being the data collector yourself.

As discussed in the chapter on subscriptions, they not only give you a recurring revenue stream, they also let you continuously learn from customers.

That learning can then lead to product improvements or adjacent products that are close to a sure thing as you can get because you already "know" the customer will like. A product that gets better as it gets older is a pretty amazing thing, but that is precisely what connected products can do.

Siginfy (the former Philips Lighting) just signed a long-term agreement with Amsterdam's Schiphol Airport. Their contract is to supply LIGHT, not light bulbs!

That not only changed their revenue model, they changed their incentives and outcomes. Since Signify now wants lights to last as long as possible, they have economic incentives to add features like Wi-Fi, smart speakers, security, and other data-based products to what used to be a plain old light bulb.

Signify smart lights tell grocery managers when products are out of stock, ping customers with smartphone offers, and show retailers heat maps of customer journeys. The incentives don't stop there. Since Signify is selling "light," they also want to save energy and recycle the product at end of life.

BTW this is an example of another new business model, CBM, the Circular Business Model. Its attributes are: employing fewer materials in producing products, extending the useful life of products, and closing the loop by recycling and reusing the product's materials again.

These multiple payoffs and applications are good for Signify's bottom line and for all of us as well.

Look at the positive ripple effect of that disruption. Smart products change how organizations operate – for good. For example:

- Sales has to learn how to sell outcomes
- IT becomes externally focused creating customer facing products rather than improving internal systems.
- Manufacturing must design simultaneously longer lasting and more complex products.

These are just a few of the puzzle pieces that can help you assemble the smart 21st century products that build "moats" to protect your franchise.

You are undoubtedly familiar with Charles Darwin's famous observation that, "It is not the strongest of the species that survives, nor the most intelligent. It is the one that is most adaptable to change."

You may be tempted to roll your eyes and think, "I've seen that a hundred times before."

That may be true. However, please look at that quote again and really think about it.

Your company may currently be strong and it may be run by intelligent executives.

The question is, are you adaptable enough to change?

Even more importantly, are you proactively preparing for change?

If so, well done. You are your company are more likely to survive and maybe even thrive.

CONCLUSION

It's time to look closely at your company's radar screen and see who is inbound.

Don't assume, as that lieutenant did, that it is a friendly (i.e., a group of US B24 bombers). Assume it is something you do not expect (like Japanese Zeros).

We've discussed dozens of technologies you can deploy, and a variety of organizational and behavioral changes you can adopt.

My hope is that they help you see incoming disruptive strikes so you're better prepared to deal with them.

You can also prevent disruptive strikes by asking yourself:

What would our company be like if?

- Netflix ran our personalization?
- Amazon ran our logistics?
- Nest did our design?
- Tesla did our advertising (by the way, they don't have any)?

Why don't we have?

- Customer reviews?
- Video explainers of our products?
- Connected products? (We can't learn or update)

Why do we have?

- Dealers? (Airlines ditched travel agents)
- A helpdesk? (Kayak doesn't)
- Such long lead times? (When people want two-day everything)
- Customers who make YouTube videos to explain our complicated product

Could we?

- Unbundle? (Music by the song)
- Lose most assets? (Uber)
- Rebuild the core for speed? (Quicken mortgage in 10 minutes)
- Listen to the customer's pain? (Dish network has a "find the remote" button on their DVR!)

Remember the Red Queen from *Alice in Wonderland*? She said, "Here, you see, it takes all the running you can do just to stay in the same place."

Is that your company? Are you running in place to just to keep up with the competition? Perhaps it's time to reimagine.

I saw a video the other day of an extremely fast bricklaying robot. It can lay bricks 1,000 times faster than a human bricklayer. That's cool.

At the same time I thought, "Why isn't there a way to reimagine home building to use robots with some other material?" That idea probably won't come from a brick company. Maybe it will come from someone who read this book and who has their antenna up for how to disrupt the norm so it becomes the exception, not the rule.

Henry Ford said this a hundred years ago and it's as true today as it was then. "One sees them all about – *men who do not know that yesterday is past*, who woke up this morning with last year's ideas."

Are there people in your organization who don't know yesterday is past? What are you going to do about it?

As we said at the opening of this book, disruption has been happening since the invention of the wheel.

You might have picked up this book because you're worried about new technology. You might have people in your organization who are concerned that "robots are going to take my job." You might wonder, "Is AI are going to take my company?"

I hope the dozens of success stories in this book from all types of industries have shown you that it *is* possible to be the disruptor instead of the disrupted.

Jeff Bezos says, "In today's era of volatility, there is no other way but to re-invent. The only sustainable advantage you can have over others is agility, that's it. Because nothing else is sustainable. Everything else you create, someone else will replicate."

Well said! If you want to be sustainable, don't just read this book and put it away on a shelf. Work through a chapter a week with your team. Answer the questions. Apply your insights. Reinvent your products and services and business models.

When you're finished with the book, start again. Because, as Bezos pointed out, constant reinvention is the only way to create sustainable success.

If you do that, if you continue to be open to new ideas and new ways of doing business – you will wake up tomorrow – with next year's ideas.

Remember you only call it a disruption, *because you didn't do it!*

Thanks for reading *Disruption OFF.*

If you'd like to learn more about disruption, AI, or innovation you can watch over thirty videos at www.tbjones.com.

Much more about innovation is detailed in my book, *ON Innovation,* which is available on Amazon.com.

You can join my mailing list and be informed about new books and videos at www.Tbjones.com/mailing

If you enjoyed this book please leave a review on Amazon.com or Goodreads.com.

Thanks!

ACKNOWLEDGMENTS

Any book is a collaborative effort and this is no exception.

Thanks to my editor and friend Sam Horn. Sam is an accomplished author and speaker in her own right. She helped me find my voice and turned a manuscript into a book. Thank you Sam!

In particular I'd like to thank my agent, Monique Boucher for reading and improving my ideas and my brother Photographer and Author Dewitt Jones who never fails to find another lens to focus on a problem.

Thanks to BookBaby for making book publishing as easy as buying a ticket on Kayak.

The ideas in this book came from thousands of interactions with speaking clients, startups and working with large corporations, but the conclusions and recommendations are my own.

And finally, thanks to all the great people I've had the privilege to work with in all the companies I've been associated with over the years. You taught me all I know about innovation and disruption.

ABOUT THE AUTHOR

Terry Jones is a serial entrepreneur, the founder of Travelocity.com and the founding Chairman of Kayak.com.

He has led four startups and served on seventeen corporate boards.

For the last fifteen years he's been speaking and consulting with companies on Innovation and Disruption.

He began his career as a travel agent, jumped to two startups and then spent twenty years at American Airlines, serving in a variety of management positions including Chief Information Officer.

While at American he led the team that created Travelocity.com and served as CEO for six years and took the company public.

After Travelocity he served as Chairman of Kayak for seven years until it was told to Priceline for $1.8 Billion.

Terry graduated from Denison University (in History).

Today in addition to speaking and consulting he is proud to be chairman of The Camping and Education Foundation whose camps get over five hundred kids into the wilderness each summer.

He divides his time between Lake Tahoe, San Clemente, California and seat 5E on American Airlines.

WANT TERRY TO SPEAK TO YOUR GROUP?

Terry is an accomplished speaker with over twenty years of onstage experience. He's spoken to tens of thousands of people worldwide.

Today his topics include:

- *ON Innovation* – building innovation in you culture, teams and organization.

- *Disruption OFF* – disruptive technologies and business models and how to adopt and adapt to them

- *Building Digital Relationships* – how to build lasting customer relationships in an increasingly complex digital world.

- *Demystifying AI* – How does AI work? Why is it important now? What are the pitfalls to avoid and strategies to adopt when deploying AI?

"You brought so much passion and energy to our event in New York. I am certain our program in France will be all the more successful for your participation."

Ginni Rometty, CEO, IBM

"Our partners have new energy and focus on innovation for our firm and our industry after listening to Terry.

Mike McGuire, CEO, Grant Thornton

To learn more about having Terry speak to your group and to watch videos of his performances go to www.tbjones.com

END NOTES:

Many of the stories in this book were told to me in the first person during consulting assignments or after speaking engagements, and for those I show no source.

In my thinking, footnotes are from a time gone by. A time when you had to go to the library and look in the card catalog to find the article or book cited. So if there is a statistic that you can easily find on the Internet, I'm not going to leave a citation here (sorry).

I have cited some specific magazines where I have gathered information and websites where they are hard to find, but you can find the issues yourself online.

Where I have quoted books, extensively, you will find their citations below.

1   Evonomics
2   The Verge
3   Wall Street Journal
4   Satya Nadella, *Hit Refresh* (HarperCollins, New York)
5   Marc Benihoff, *Beyond the Cloud* (Jossey-Bass, San Francisco)
6   Cat.com
7   Reid Hoffman & Chris Yeh, *Blitzscaling* (Crown Publishing, New York)
8   Cleverism.com
9   Whitlock

10 Wired Magazine

11 Harvard Business Review

12 Advisory.com

13 USA Today

14 Taskandpurpose.com

15 Uploader.vr

16 Youtube

17 Statistica

18 SAS Institute

19 CNN

20 London Business School

21 Tien Tzou, *Subscribed* (Penguin, New York)

22 Ibid

23 ECIS 2015 Proceedings Digitizitaions and Path Disruption

24 Harvard Business Review

25 Gillian Tett, *The Silo Effect* (Simon & Schuster, New York)

26 Ed Catmull & Amy Wallace, *Creativity, Inc.* (Random House, New York)

27 New York Times

28 John Chambers, *Connecting the Dots* (Hachette, New York)

29 Innovation Leader Report on Innovation

30 Chambers (xxvii)

31 Fast Company

32 Equipment World

33 Fastcompany

34 Charles Koch, *Good Profit* (Random House, New York)

35 James Brown, *The Boys in the Boat* (Penguin, New York)

36 Harvard Business Review